BOOK OF THE FEET:

A

HISTORY OF BOOTS AND SHOES,

𝕎𝕚𝕥𝕙 𝕀𝕝𝕝𝕦𝕤𝕥𝕣𝕒𝕥𝕚𝕠𝕟𝕤

OF THE

FASHIONS OF THE EGYPTIANS, HEBREWS, PERSIANS, GREEKS, AND
ROMANS, AND THE PREVAILING STYLE THROUGHOUT EUROPE,
DURING THE MIDDLE AGES, DOWN TO THE PRESENT PERIOD;

ALSO,

HINTS TO LAST-MAKERS, AND REMEDIES FOR CORNS, ETC.

BY J. SPARKES HALL,

Patent-Elastic-Boot Maker to her Majesty the Queen, the Queen Dowager,
and the Queen of the Belgians.

FROM THE SECOND LONDON EDITION,

WITH A HISTORY OF BOOTS AND SHOES IN THE UNITED STATES,

BIOGRAPHICAL SKETCHES OF EMINENT SHOEMAKERS,

AND CRISPIN ANECDOTES.

Leather Crafting

Leather is a durable and flexible material created by the tanning of animal rawhide and skin, often cattle hide. It can be produced through manufacturing processes ranging from cottage industry to heavy industry, and has formed a central part of the dress and useful accessories of many cultures around the world. Leather has played an important role in the development of civilisation from prehistoric times to the present, and people have used the skins of animals to satisfy fundamental (as well as not so essential!) needs such as clothing, shelter, carpets and even decorative attire. As a result of this importance, decorating leather has become a large past time. Leather crafting or simply leathercraft is the practice of making leather into craft objects or works of art, using shaping techniques, colouring techniques or both. Today, it is a global past time.

Some of the main techniques of leather crafting include:

Dyeing - which usually involves the use of spirit- or alcohol-based dyes where alcohol quickly gets absorbed into moistened leather, carrying the pigment deep into the surface. 'Hi-liters' and 'Antiquing' stains can be used to add more definition to patterns. These have pigments that will break away from the higher points of a tooled piece and so pooling in the background areas give nice contrasts. This leaves parts unstained and also provides a type of contrast.

Painting - This differs from leather dyeing, in that paint remains only on the surface whilst dyes are absorbed into the leather. Due to this difference, leather painting techniques are generally not used on items that can or must bend, nor on items that receive friction, such as belts and wallets - as under these conditions, the paint is likely to crack and flake off. However, latex paints can be used to paint flexible leather items. In the main though, a flat piece of leather, backed with a stiff board is ideal and common, though three-dimensional forms are possible so long as the painted surface remains secured. Unlike photographs, leather paintings are displayed without a glass cover, to prevent mould.

Stamping - Leather stamping involves the use of shaped implements (stamps) to create an imprint onto a leather surface, often by striking the stamps with a mallet. Commercial stamps are available in various designs, typically geometric or representative of animals. Most stamping is performed on vegetable tanned leather that has been dampened with water, as the water makes the leather softer and able to be compressed with the design. After the leather has been stamped, the design stays on the leather as it dries out, but it can fade if the leather becomes wet and is flexed. To make the impressions last longer, the leather is conditioned with oils and fats to make it waterproof and prevent the fibres from deforming.

Molding and shaping - Leather shaping or molding consists of soaking a piece of leather in hot or room temperature water to greatly increase pliability and then shaping it by hand or with the use of objects or even molds as forms. As the leather dries it stiffens and holds its shape. Carving and stamping may be done prior to molding. Dying however, must take place after molding, as the water soak will remove much of the colour. This mode of leather crafting has become incredibly popular among hobbyists whose crafts are related to fantasy, goth / steampunk culture and cosplay.

A History of Shoemaking

Shoemaking, at its simplest, is the process of making footwear. Whilst the art has now been largely superseded by mass-volume industrial production, for most of history, making shoes was an individual, artisanal affair. 'Shoemakers' or 'cordwainers' (cobblers being those who repair shoes) produce a range of footwear items, including shoes, boots, sandals, clogs and moccasins – from a vast array of materials.

When people started wearing shoes, there were only three main types: open sandals, covered sandals and clog-like footwear. The most basic foot protection, used since ancient times in the Mediterranean area, was the sandal, which consisted of a protective sole, attached to the foot with leather thongs. Similar footwear worn in the Far East was made from plaited grass or palm fronds. In climates that required a full foot covering, a single piece of untanned hide was laced with a thong, providing full protection for the foot, thus forming a complete covering. These were the main two types of footwear, produced all over the globe. The production of wooden shoes was mainly limited to medieval Europe however – made from a single piece of wood, roughly shaped to fit the foot.

A variant of this early European shoe was the clog, which were wooden soles to which a leather upper was attached. The sole and heel were generally made from one piece of maple or ash two inches thick, and a little longer and broader than the desired size of shoe. The outer side of the sole and heel was fashioned with a long chisel-edged implement, called the clogger's knife or stock; while a second implement, called the groover, made a groove around the side of the sole. With the use of a 'hollower', the inner sole's contours were adapted to the shape of the foot. In even colder climates, such designs were adapted with furs wrapped around the feet, and then sandals wrapped over them. The Romans used such footwear to great effect whilst fighting in Northern Europe, and the native Indians developed similar variants with their ubiquitous moccasin.

By the 1600s, leather shoes came in two main types. 'Turn shoes' consisted of one thin flexible sole, which was sewed to the upper while outside in and turned over when completed. This type was used for making slippers and similar shoes. The second type united the upper with an insole, which was subsequently attached to an out-sole with a raised heel. This was the main variety, and was used for most footwear, including standard shoes and riding boots.

Shoemaking became more commercialized in the mid-eighteenth century, as it expanded as a cottage industry. Large warehouses began to stock footwear made by many small manufacturers from the area. Until the nineteenth century, shoemaking was largely a traditional handicraft, but by the century's end, the process had been almost completely mechanized, with production occurring in large factories. Despite the obvious economic gains of mass-production, the factory system produced shoes without the individual differentiation that the traditional shoemaker was able to provide.

The first steps towards mechanisation were taken during the Napoleonic Wars by the English engineer, Marc Brunel. He developed machinery for the mass-production of boots for the soldiers of the British Army. In 1812 he devised a scheme for making nailed-boot-making machinery that automatically fastened soles to uppers by means of metallic pins or nails. With the support of the Duke of York, the shoes were manufactured, and, due to their strength, cheapness, and durability, were introduced for the use of the army. In the same year, the use of screws and staples was patented by Richard Woodman. However, when the war ended in 1815, manual labour became much cheaper again, and the demand for military equipment subsided. As a consequence, Brunel's system was no longer profitable and it soon ceased business.

Similar exigencies at the time of the Crimean War stimulated a renewed interest in methods of mechanization and mass-production, which proved longer lasting. A shoemaker in Leicester, Tomas Crick, patented the design for a riveting machine in 1853. He also introduced the use of steam-powered rolling-machines for hardening leather and cutting-machines, in the mid-1850s. Another important factor in shoemaking's mechanization, was the introduction of the sewing machine in 1846 – a development which revolutionised so many aspects of clothes, footwear and domestic production.

By the late 1850s, the industry was beginning to shift towards the modern factory, mainly in the US and areas of England. A shoe stitching machine was invented by the American Lyman Blake in 1856 and perfected by 1864.

Entering in to partnership with Gordon McKay, his device became known as the McKay stitching machine and was quickly adopted by manufacturers throughout New England. As bottlenecks opened up in the production line due to these innovations, more and more of the manufacturing stages, such as pegging and finishing, became automated. By the 1890s, the process of mechanisation was largely complete.

Traditional shoemakers still exist today, especially in poorer parts of the world, and do continue to create custom shoes. In more economically developed countries however, it is a dying craft. Despite this, the shoemaking profession makes a number of appearances in popular culture, such as in stories about shoemaker's elves (written by the Brothers Grimm in 1806), and the old proverb that 'the shoemaker's children go barefoot.' Chefs and cooks sometimes use the term 'shoemaker' as an insult to others who have prepared sub-standard food, possibly by overcooking, implying that the chef in question has made his or her food as tough as shoe leather or hard leather shoe soles. Similarly, reflecting the trade's humble beginnings, to 'cobble' can mean not only to make or mend shoes, but 'to put together clumsily; or, to bungle.'

As is evident from this short introduction, 'shoemaking' has a long and varied history, starting from a simple means of providing basic respite from the elements, to a fully mechanised and modern, global trade. It is able to provide a fascinating insight not only into fashion, but society, culture and climate more generally. We hope the reader enjoys this book.

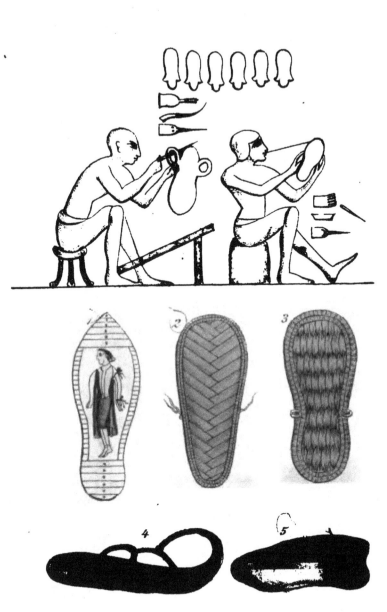

Pl.1.

AMERICAN PREFACE.

THE work embraced in the following pages, which has been received with great favor in England, in the fashionable circles, as well as by the trade, the publisher has great confidence will prove attractive and interesting to the American public.

"I have given," says Mr. Hall, in his preface to the English edition, "the result of my experience, derived from an intimate practical acquaintance with this department of trade for twenty years, and have endeavored to correct much that was bad in form and material, and I trust have not only found fault in many instances with past and present fashions, but have also enforced and provided the remedy. The illustrations of the ancient fashions are all taken from the highest authorities, and I believe may be relied on as historical."

In addition to the matter in the second London edition, we have subjoined a History of Boots and Shoes in the United States, showing the changes of fashion in this indispensable article of dress; also, numerous biographical sketches of individuals, who, having learned the art of shoemaking, have afterward distinguished themselves by their genius, talents, or worth, and occupied eminent stations among their fellow-men.

The frequency of the development of literary talent among shoemakers has often been remarked. Their occupation, being a sedentary and comparatively noiseless one, may be considered as more favorable than some others to meditation; but perhaps its literary productiveness has arisen quite as much from the circumstance of its being a trade of light labor, and therefore resorted to, in preference to most others, by persons in humble life who are conscious of more mental talent than bodily strength.

To add further to the interest of this volume, we have selected a few pages of anecdotes, and other miscellaneous matters, tending to elucidate this

History and account of the "gentle craft;" the members of which may well be proud of such names as their Sherman, Drew, Bloomfield, Gifford, Lee, Sheffey, Worcester, and others, whose memory will long live, as having adorned the various pursuits in which they became eminent.

While this work will prove useful and instructive as presenting, in the biographical sketches, a body of examples showing, how the most unpropitious circumstances have been unable to subdue an ardent desire for the acquisition of knowledge, and the cultivation of a refined taste; the lover of antiquities, and the votary of fashion, will here have their curiosity gratified, in a history of the varied changes which have taken place in an important article of dress, from the pyramidal ages of ancient Egypt, long ere Greece or Rome occupied a space in history, to the present time, when the beauty, taste, and convenience, of modern boots and shoes, combine to establish the superiority of the cordwainers of Europe and America, compared with their predecessors of any nation or age.

1*

CONTENTS.

HISTORY OF BOOTS AND SHOES.

CHAPTER I.

ON THE MOST ANCIENT COVERINGS FOR THE FEET.

IF we investigate the monuments of the remotest nations of antiquity, we shall find that the earliest form of protection for the feet, partook of the nature of sandals. The most ancient representations we possess of scenes in ordinary life, are the sculptures and paintings of early Egypt, and these the investigations of travelled scholars from most modern civilized countries have, by their descriptions and delineations, made familiar to us, so that the habits and manners, as well as the costume of this ancient people, have been handed down to the present time, by the work of their own hands, with so vivid a truthfulness, that we feel as conversant with their domestic manners and customs, as with those of any modern nation to which the book of

the traveller would introduce us.   Not only do their
pictured relics remain to give us an insight into
their mode of life, but a vast quantity of articles of
all kinds, from the tools of the workmen, to the
elegant fabrics which once decorated the boudoir
of the fair ladies of Memphis and .Carnac three
thousand years ago, are treasured up in the mu-
seums, both public and private, of this and other
countries.

  With these materials, it is in no wise difficult to
carry our history of shoemaking back to the earliest
times, and even to look upon the shoemaker at his
work, in the early days of Thothmes the third, who
ascended the throne of Egypt, according to Wilkinson, 1495 years before Christ, and during whose
reign, the Exodus of the Israelites occurred.   The
first of our plates contains a copy of this very curious painting, as it existed upon the walls of Thebes,
when the Italian scholar Rossellini copied it for
his great work on Egypt.   The shoemakers are
both seated upon low stools (real specimens of such
articles may be seen in the British Museum), and
are both busily employed, in the formation of the
sandals then usually worn in Egypt, the first workman is piercing with his awl the leather thong, at
the side of the sole, through which the straps were
passed, which secured the sandal to the foot; be-

fore him is a low sloping bench, one end of which rests upon the ground; his fellow-workman is equally busy, sewing a shoe, and tightening the thong with his teeth, a primitive mode of working which is occasionally indulged in at the present day. Above their heads is a goodly row of sandals, probably so placed, to attract a passing customer; the shops in the East being then, as now, entirely open and exposed to every one who passed. As the ancient Egyptian artists knew nothing of perspective, the tools of the workmen that lie around, are here represented above them: they bear, in some instances, a resemblance to those used in the present day; the central instrument, above the man who pierces the tie of the sandal, having the precise shape of the shoemaker's awl still in use, so very unchanging are articles of utility. In the same manner, the semicircular knife used by the ancient Egyptians three or four thousand years ago, is precisely similar to that of our modern curriers, and is thus represented in a

painting at Thebes, of that remote antiquity. The workman, it will be noticed, cuts the leather upon a sloping bench, exactly like that of the shoemaker already engraved.

The warmth and mildness of the East, rendered a close, warm shoe unnecessary; and, indeed, in the present day, they partake there more of the character of slippers; and the foot, thus unconfined by tight shoes, and always free in its motion, retained its full power and pliability: and the custom, still retained in the East, of holding a strap of leather, or other substance, between the toes, is represented in the Theban paintings; the foot thus becoming a useful second to the hand.

Many specimens of the shoes and sandals of the ancient Egyptians, may be seen in our national museum. Wilkinson, in his work on the "Manners and Customs" of this people says, "Ladies and men of rank paid great attention to the beauty of their sandals: but on some occasions, those of the middle classes who were in the habit of wearing them, preferred walking barefooted; and in religious ceremonies, the priests frequently took them off while performing their duties in the temple."

The sandals varied slightly in form; those worn by the upper classes, and by women, were usually pointed and turned up at the end, like our skates, and the Eastern slippers of the present day. Some had a sharp flat point, others were nearly round. They were made of a sort of woven or interlaced work, of palm leaves and papyrus stalks, or other similar materials; sometimes of leather, and were frequently lined within with cloth, on which the figure of a captive was painted; that humiliating position being thought suitable to the enemies of their country, whom they hated and despised, an idea agreeing perfectly with the expression which so often occurs in the hieroglyphic legends, accompanying a king's name, where his valor and virtues are recorded on the sculptures : "you have trodden the impure Gentiles under your powerful feet."

The example selected for pl. I., fig. 1, is in the British Museum, beneath the sandal of a mummy of Harsontiotf; and the captive figure is evidently, from feature and costume, a Jew : it thus becomes a curious illustration of scripture history.

Upon the same plate, figs. 3 and 4 delineate two fine examples of sandals formed as above described, of the leaf of the palm. They were brought from Egypt by the late Mr. Salt, consul-general, and formed part of the collection sold in London, after his death, and are now in the British Museum. They are very different to each other in their construction, and are of that kind worn by the poorer classes; flat slices of the palm leaf, which lap over each other in the centre, form the sole of fig. 2, and a double band of twisted leaves secures and strengthens the edge; a thong of the strong fibres of the same plant is affixed to each side of the instep, and was secured round the foot. The other (fig. 3) is more elaborately platted, and has a softer look; it must in fact have been as a pad to the foot, exceedingly light and agreeable in the arid climate inhabited by the people for whom such sandals were constructed; the knot at each side to which the thong was affixed, still remains.

The sandals with curved toes, alluded to above, and which frequently appear upon Egyptian sculpture, and generally upon the feet of the superior classes, are exhibited in the woodcut here given:

and in the Berlin museum, one is preserved of precisely similar form, which has been engraved by Wilkinson, and is here copied, pl. I., fig. 1. It is particularly curious, as showing how such sandals were held upon the feet, the thong which crosses the instep being connected with another, passing

over the top of the foot and secured to the sole,
between the great toe and that next to it, so that
the sole was held firmly, however the foot moved,
and yet it allowed the sandal to be cast off at
pleasure.

Wilkinson says that "shoes or low boots, were
also common in Egypt, but these I believe to have
been of late date, and to have belonged to Greeks;
for since no persons are represented in the paintings wearing them, except foreigners, we may conclude they were not adopted by the Egyptians, at
least in a Pharaonic age. They were of leather,
generally of green color, laced in front by thongs,
which passed through small loops on either side;
and were principally used, as in Greece and
Etruria, by women."

One of the close-laced shoes is given in pl. I.,
fig. 4, from a specimen in the British museum. It
embraces the foot closely, and has a thong or two
over the instep, for drawing it tightly over the foot,
something like the half-boot of the present day.
The sole and upper leather are all in one piece,
sewn up the back and down the front of the foot;
a mode of construction practised in England, as
late as the fourteenth century.

The elegantly-ornamented boot here given, is
copied from a Theban painting, and is worn by a

2

gayly-dressed youth from one of the countries bordering on Egypt: it reaches very high, and is a remarkable specimen of the taste for decoration, which thus early began to be displayed upon this article of apparel.

In Sacred Writ are many early notices of shoes, when Moses exhorts the Jews to obedience (Deut. ch. xxix.), he exclaims, "Your clothes are not waxen old upon you, and thy shoe is not waxen old upon thy foot." In the book of Ruth (chap. iv.) we have a curious instance of the important part performed by the shoe in the ancient days of Israel, in sealing any important business: "Now this was the manner in former time in Israel, concerning redeeming, and concerning changing, for to confirm all things; a man plucked off his shoe, and gave it to his neighbor; and this was a testimony in Israel." Ruth, and all the property of three other persons, are given over to Boaz, by the act of the next kinsman, who gives to him his shoe in the presence of

witnesses. The ancient law compelled the eldest
brother, or nearest kinsman by her late husband's
side, to marry a widow, if her husband died child-
less. The law of Moses provided an alternative,
easy in itself, but attended with some degree of
ignominy. The woman was in public court to take
off his shoe, spit before his face, saying, "so shall
it be done unto that man that will not build up his
brother's house:" and probably, the fact of this re-
fusal was stated in the genealogical registers in
connexion with his name; which is probably what
is meant by his "name shall be called in Israel, the
house of him that hath his shoe loosed." (Deut.
xxv.) The editor of Knight's Pictorial Bible, who
notices these curious laws, also adds that the use
of the shoe in the transactions with Boaz, are perfectly intelligible; the taking off the shoe, deno-
ting the relinquishment of the right, and the disso-
lution of the obligation in the one instance, and its
transfer in the other. The shoe is regarded as con-
stituting possession, nor is this idea unknown to
ourselves, in being conveyed in the homely proverbial expression by which one man is said to "stand
in the shoes of another," and the vulgar idea of
"throwing an old shoe after you for luck," is typi-
cal of a wish, that temporal gifts or good fortune
may follow you. The author last quoted says, that

even at the present time, the use of the shoe as a
token of right or occupancy, may be traced very
extensively in the East; and however various and
dissimilar the instances may seem at first view, the
leading idea may be still detected in all. Thus
among the Bedouins, when a man permits his
cousin to marry another, or when a husband di-
vorces his runaway wife, he usually says, "She
was my slipper, I have cast her off." (Burck-
hardt's "Bedouins," p. 65.) Sir F. Henniker, in
speaking of the difficulty he had in persuading
the natives to descend into the crocodile mummy
pits, in consequence of some men having lost
their lives there, says: "Our guides, as if preparing for certain death, took leave of their children; the father took the turban from his own
head, and put it upon that of his son; or *put him
in his place*, by giving him *his shoes*, 'a dead man's
shoes.'" In western Asia, slippers left at the door
of an apartment, denote that the master or mistress is engaged, and no one ventures on intru-
sion, not even a husband, though the apartment
be his wife's. Messrs. Tyerman and Bennet,
speaking of the termagants of Benares, say, "If
domestic or other business calls off one of the
combatants before the affair is duly settled, she
coolly thrusts *her shoe* beneath her basket, and

leaves both upon the spot, to signify that she is not satisfied;" meaning to denote by leaving her shoe, that she kept possession of the ground and the argument during her unavoidable absence.

From all these instances, it would appear that this employment of the shoe, may, in some respects, be considered analogous to that which prevailed in the middle ages, of giving a glove as a token of investiture, when bestowing lands and dignities.

It should be observed that the same Hebrew word (*naal*), signifies both a sandal and a shoe, although always rendered shoe in our translation of the Old Testament. Although the shoe is mentioned in Genesis and other books of the Bible, little concerning its form or manufacture can be gleaned—that it was an article of common use among the ancient Israelites, we may infer from the passage in Genesis, chap. xiv., verse 23, the first mention we have of this article, where Abraham makes oath to the king of Sodom "that he will not take from a thread even to a shoe-latchet," thus assuming its common character.

The Gibeonites (Josh. ix. 5–13) " came with old shoes and clouted [mended] upon their feet"—the better to practise their deceit; and therefore they

2*

said, "Our shoes are become old by reason of the very long journey."

Isaiah "walked three years naked and barefoot:" he went for this long period without shoes, contrary to the custom of the people, and as "a wonder unto Egypt and Ethiopia."

That it became an article of refinement and luxury, is evident from the many other notices given; and the Jewish ladies seem to have been very particular about their sandals : thus we are told, in the Apocryphal book of Judith, although Holofernes was attracted by the general richness of her dress and personal ornaments, yet it was "her sandals ravished his eyes :" and the bride in Solomon's Song is met with the exclamation, "How beautiful are thy feet with sandals, O prince's daughter !"

The ancient bas-reliefs at Persepolis, and the neighborhood of Babylon, second only in their antiquity and interest to those of Egypt, furnish us with examples of the boots and shoes of the Persian kings, their nobles, and attendants ; and they were executed, as appears from historical, as well as internal evidence, in the days of Xerxes and Darius.

From these sources, we here select the three following specimens. No. 1 is a half-boot, reaching considerably above the ankle ; and it is worn by

No. 1,   No. 2.   No. 3.

the attendant who has charge of a chariot, upon a
bas-relief now in the British museum, brought
from Persepolis by Sir R. Ker Porter, by whom it
was first engraved and described in his interesting
volumes of travels in that district. No. 2, also
from Persepolis, and engraved in the work just
quoted, delineates another kind of boot, or high
shoe, reaching only to the ankle, round which it is
secured by a band, and tied in front in a knot, the
two ends of the band hanging beneath it. This
shoe is very common upon the feet of these figures,
and is generally worn by soldiers or the upper
classes: the attendants or councillors round the
throne of these early sovereigns, frequently wear
such shoes. No. 3, seen upon the feet of personages in the same rank of life, is here copied from
a Persepolitan bas-relief, representing a soldier in
full costume. It is a remarkably interesting example, as it very clearly shows the transition state
of this article of dress, being something between a
shoe and a sandal : in fact, a shoe may be considered as a covered sandal ; and, in the instance be-

fore us, the part we now term "upper leather"
consists of little more than the lacings of the sandals, rendered much broader than usual, and fastened by buttons along the top of the foot. The
shoe is thus rendered peculiarly flexible, as the
openings over the instep allow of the freest move-
ment. Such were the forms of the earliest shoes.

Close boots reaching nearly to the knee where
they are met by a wide trowser, are not uncommon
upon these sculptures, being precisely the same in
shape and appearance as those worn by the modern
Cossacks. Indeed, there is nothing in the way of
boots that may not be found upon the existing monuments of early nations, precisely resembling the
modern ones. The little figure here given might

pass for a copy of the boots worn by one of the
soldiers of King William the Third's army, and

would not be unworthy of uncle Toby himself, yet it is carefully copied from a most ancient specimen of Etruscan sculpture, in the possession of Inghirami, who has engraved it in his learned work the "Monumenti Etruschi;" the original represents an augur, or priest, whose chief duty was to report and explain supernatural signs.

With the ancient Greeks and Romans; the coverings for the feet assumed their most elegant forms; yet in no instance does the comfort of the wearer appear to have been sacrificed, or the natural play of the foot interfered with — *that* appears to have been especially reserved for "march-of-intellect" days. Vegetable sandals, termed Baxa, or Baxea, were worn by the lower classes, and as a symbol of their humility, by the philosophers and priests. Apuleius describes a young priest as wearing sandals of palm; they were no doubt similar in construction to the Egyptian ones, of which we have already given specimens, and which were part of the required and characteristic dress of the Egyptian priesthood. Such vegetable sandals were, however, occasionally decorated with ornaments to a considerable extent, and they then became expensive. The making of them in all their variety, was the business of a class of men called Baxearii; and these with the Solearii (or makers of the sim-

plest kind of sandal worn, consisting of a sole
with little more to fasten it to the foot than a strap
across the instep) constituted a corporation or
college of Rome.

The solea were generally worn by the higher
classes only, for lightness and convenience, in the
house; the shoes (calceus) being worn out of doors.
The soccus was the intermediate covering for the
foot, being something between the solea and the
calceus; it was, in fact, precisely like the modern
slipper, and could be cast of at pleasure, as it did
not fit closely, and was secured by no tie. This,
like the solea and crepida, was worn by the lower
classes and country people; and hence, the come-
dians wore such cheap and common coverings for
the feet, to contrast with the cothurnus or buskin
of the tragedians, which they assumed, as it was
adapted to be part of a grand and stately attire.
Hence the term applied to theatrical performers—
"brethren of the sock and buskin," and as this
distinction is both ancient and curious, specimens
of both are here given from antique authorities.
The side and front views of the sock (Nos. 1, 2)
are copied from a painting of a buffoon, who is dan-
cing in loose yellow slippers, one of the common-
est colors in which the leather used for their construction was dyed. Such slippers were made to

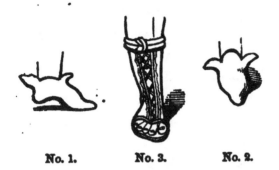

No. 1.   No. 3.   No. 2.

fit both feet indifferently, but the more finished
boots and shoes were made for one foot only from
the earliest period. The cothurnus (fig. 3) was a
boot of the highest kind, reaching above the calf
of the leg, and sometimes as far as the knee. It
was laced as the boots of the ancients always were,
down the front, the object of such an arrangement
being to make them fit the leg as closely as possible, and the skin of which they were made was
dyed purple, and other gay colors; the head and
paws of the wild animal were sometimes allowed
to hang around the leg from the upper part of the
cothurnus, to which it formed a graceful addition;
an example is given upon our 2d plate, fig. 1,
which is a side-view of such an ornamented boot,
decorated all over with a pattern like the Grecian
volute.

The sole of the cothurnus was of the ordinary
thickness in general, but it was occasionally made

much thicker by the insertion of slices of cork when the wearer wished to add to his height, and thus the Athenian tragedians, who assumed this boot as the most dignified of coverings for the feet, had the soles made unusually thick, in order that it might add to the magnitude and dignity of their whole appearance.

The unchanging nature of a commodious fashion capable of adoption by the lower classes, may be well illustrated by fig. 2, plate II., which delineates the shoe or sandal worn by the rustics of ancient Rome. It is formed of a skin turned over the foot, and secured by thongs passing through the sides, and over the toe, crossing each other over the instep, and secured firmly round the ankle. Any person familiar with the prints of Pinelli, pictures of the modern brigands of the Abruzzi, or the models of the latter worthies in terra-cotta, to be met with in most curiosity-shops, will at once recognise those they wear as being of the same form. The traveller who has visited modern Rome, will also remember to have seen them on the feet of the peasantry who traverse the Pontine marshes; and the older Irish, and the comparatively modern Highlander, both wore similar ones; they were formed of the skin of the cow or deer, with the hair on them, and were held on the feet by

Pl. 2.

leather thongs. They were the simplest and warmest kind of foot-covering to be obtained, when every man was his own shoemaker.

There was a form of shoe worn at this early time, in which the toes were entirely uncovered, and of which an example is given in plate II., fig. 3. It is copied from a marble foot in the British museum. This shoe appears to be made of a pliable leather, which fits closely to the foot, for it was considered as a mark of rusticity to wear shoes larger than the foot, or which fitted in a loose and slovenly manner. The toes in this instance are left perfectly free; the upper leather is secured round the ankle by a tie, while a thong, ornamented by a stud in its centre, passing over the instep, and between the great and second toes, is secured to the sole in the manner of a sandal. In order that the ankle-bone should not be pressed on or incommoded in walking, the leather is sloped away, and rises around it to a point at the back of the leg.

None but such as had served the office of edile were allowed to wear shoes of a red color, which we may therefore infer to have been a favorite color for shoes, as it appears to have been among the Hebrews, and as it is still in western Asia. The Roman senators wore shoes or buskins of a black color, with a crescent of gold or silver on the top

of the foot. The emperor Aurelian forbade men
to wear red, yellow, white, or green shoes, permit-
ting them to be worn by women only, and Heliogabalus forbade women to wear gold or precious
stones in their shoes, a fact which will aid us in
understanding the sort of decoration indulged in
by the earliest Hebrew women, of whose example
Judith may be quoted as an instance, to which we
have already referred.

The Roman soldiers generally wore a simple
form of sandal similar to the example given in plate
II., fig. 4, and which is a solea fastened by thongs;
yet they, in the progress of riches and luxury,
went with the times and merged into foppery, so
that Philopoemon, in recommending soldiers to
give more attention to their warlike accoutrements
than to their common dress, advises them to be less
nice about their shoes and sandals, and more care-
ful in observing that their greaves were kept bright
and fitted well to their legs. When about to at-
tack a hill-fort or go on rugged marches, they wore
a sandal shod with spikes similar to that in plate II.,
fig. 5, and at other times they had soles covered
with large clumsy nails like those of fig. 6, which
exhibits the sole of a Roman soldier's sandal, covered with nails, and which was discovered in London some few years ago; it is copied from an en-

graving in the Archæological album, and the shoe itself, which forms fig. 7, shows the length of these nails, and the way in which the upper leather was constructed of the sandal form, like those of the Persepolitan figures already alluded to. The Greeks and Romans used shoes of this kind as frequently as the early Persians, and in fig. 7, we have an example of such a combination of sandal and shoe as they wore, the upper leather being cut into a series of thongs, through which passes a broad band of leather, which turns not inelegantly round the upper part of the foot, and is secured by passing many times round the ankle and above it, where it is buckled or tied.

The Roman shoes then had various names, and were distinct badges of the position in society held by the wearer. The solea, crepida, pero, and soccus, belonged to the lower classes, the laborers and rustics, the caliga was principally worn by soldiers, and the cothurnus by tragedians, hunters, and horsemen, as well as by the nobles of the country.

The latter kind of boot, in form and color, as we have already hinted, was indicative of rank or office. Those worn by senators we have noticed, and it was a joke in ancient Rome against a man who owed respect solely to the accident of birth or fortune, that his nobility was in his heels. The

boots of the emperors were frequently richly decorated, and the patterns still existing upon marble
statues, show that they were ornamented in the
most elaborate manner. A specimen from the noble statue of Hadrian in the British museum,
forms fig. 8, of our plate, and it is impossible to
conceive anything of the kind more elegant and
tasteful in its decorations. Real gems and gold
were employed by some of the Roman emperors to
decorate their boots, and Heliogabalus wore exquisite cameos on his boots and shoes. Fig. 9, is a
lower kind of boot, of the same make as fig. 3, but
beautifully ornamented.

The Grecian ladies, according to Hope, wore
shoes or half-boots, laced before and lined with the
fur of animals of the cat tribe, whose muzzles or
claws hung down from the top.

Ocrea was the name this boot got among the
Romans; " *Ocreas verdente puella*," (Juv. vi. sat.);
which Dryden, ridiculously enough, translated
"Spanish leather boots," a term of his own time,
forced to do service sixteen hundred years before.

The barbarous nations with whom the Romans
held war, are upon the bas-reliefs of their conquer-
ors, represented in close shoes or half-boots. Thus
the Dacians wear the shoe represented in fig. 10,
which laced across the instep, and was secured

around the ankle with a band and ornamental button or stud. The Gauls wear the shoe given below, of the same form as that worn by our native
ancestors when Julius Cæsar made his descent upon the British islands.

3*

CHAPTER II.

BEFORE the arrival of the Saxons, who have transmitted to us many valuable manuscripts abounding in various delineations of their dress and manners, we shall not find much to engage the attention where it is our present object to direct it, the history of the coverings for the feet. There is, however, little doubt that the rude skin-shoes, worn by the native Irish and the country people of Rome, was the simple protection adopted in this country in the earliest times. Shoes of this material are found in all nations half-civilized, and the ease with which they are formed by merely covering the sole with the hide of an animal, and securing it by a thong, must have had the effect of insuring its general use. Naked feet would, however, be preferred in fine weather, and when shoes were worn, they were generally of a close, warm kind, adapted to our climate; the most antique representations of the Gaulish native chiefs, as given on Roman sculpture, and which may be taken as general representations of British chiefs, may be received as good authorities, their resemblance to each other being so striking as to draw from Cæsar a remark to that effect.

The Saxon figures, as given in the drawings by their own hands, to be seen in manuscripts in most of our public libraries, display the costume of this people, from the ninth century downward; and the minute way in which every portion of the dress is given, affords us clear examples of their boots and shoes. According to Strutt, high shoes, reaching nearly to the middle of the legs, and fastened by lacing in the front, and which may also be properly considered as a species of half-boots, were in use in this country as early as the tenth century; and the only apparent difference between the high shoes of the ancients and the moderns, seems to have been that the former laced close down to the toes, and the latter to the instep only. They appear in general to have been made of leather, and were usually fastened beneath the ankles with a thong, which passed through a fold upon the upper part of the leather, encompassing the heel, and which was tied upon the instep. This method of securing the shoe upon the foot, was certainly well contrived both for ease and convenience. Three specimens of shoes are here given from Saxon

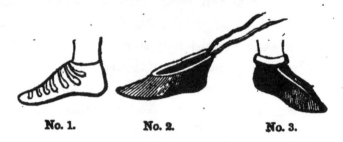

No. 1. No. 2. No. 3.

drawings. The first is the most ancient and curious; it is copied from "the Durham Book," or book of St. Cuthbert, now preserved among the Cottonian manuscripts in the British museum, and is believed to have been executed as early as the seventh century, by the hands of Eadfreid, afterward bishop of Lindisfarne, who died in 721. It partakes of the nature of shoe and sandal, and with the exception of the buttons down the front, is precisely like the Persepolitan sandal already engraved and described, as well as like the Roman ones constructed on the same model, and it is curious to see how all are formed after this one fashion.

No. 2, is copied from Strutt's "complete view of the dress and habits of the people of England," plate XXIX., fig. 16, and which he obtained from the Harleian MS., No. 603. It very clearly shows

the form of the Saxon shoe, and the long strings
by which it was tied.   Fig. 3, delineates the most
ordinary kind of shoe worn, with the opening to
the toes already alluded to, for lacing it.   But little
variety is observable in the form of this article of
dress among the Saxons; it is usually delineated as
a solid black mass, just as the last figure has been
here engraved, with a white line down the centre,
to show the opening, but quite as generally without it, and these two forms of shoe or half-boot,
are by far the most commonly met with, and are de-
picted upon the feet of noble and royal personages
as well as upon those of the lower class.

Strutt remarks that wooden shoes are mentioned
in the records of this era, but considers it probable that they were so called because the soles
were formed of wood, while the upper parts were
formed with some more pliant material: shoes
with wooden soles were at this time worn by persons of the most exalted rank; thus, the shoes of
Bernard, king of Italy the grandson of Charlemagne, are thus described by an Italian writer, as
they were found in his tomb.

"The shoes," says he, "which covered his feet
are remaining to this day, the soles of wood and
the upper parts of red leather, laced together with
thongs: they were so closely fitted to the feet that

the order of the toes, terminating in a point at the great toe, might easily be discovered; so that the shoe belonging to the right foot could not be put upon the left, nor that of the left upon the right." It was not uncommon to gild and otherwise ornament the shoes of the nobility. Eginhart describes the shoes worn by Charlemagne on great occasions, as set with jewels.

The Normans wore boots and shoes of equal simplicity, rustics are frequently represented with a half-boot plain in form, fitting close to the foot, but wide at the ankle, like fig. 1, of the group here given, only that in this instance, an ornament consisting of a studded band surrounds the upper

Fig. 1.   Fig. 2.   Fig. 3.

part. Such boots were much used by the Normans, and are frequently mentioned by the ancient historians; they do not appear to have been confined to any particular classes of the people, but were worn by persons of all ranks and conditions, as well of the clergy as of the laity, especially when they rode on horseback. The boots delineated in their drawings are very short, rarely reaching higher than the middle of the legs; they were sometimes slightly ornamented, but the boots and shoes of all personages represented in the famous tapestry of Bayeux, are of the same simple form of construction; ånd this celebrated early piece of needlework was believed to have been worked by the wife of the conqueror, to commemorate his invasion of England and the battle of Hastings. Another form of Norman shoes may be seen in fig. 2, which is more enriched than the last, and it is curious that the ornament adopted is in the form of the straps of a sandal, studded with dots throughout. In the original, the shoe is colored with a thin tint of black, these bands being a solid black, with white or gilded lines and dots. Another example of a decorated shoe, fig. 3, is given from a MS. of the eleventh century, in the British museum, and shows the kind which became fashionable when the Normans, firmly settled in England, began to indulge in luxurious clothing. These shoes were most probably embroidered.

"We are assured by the early Norman historians," says Strutt, "that the cognomen *curta ocrea*, or short boots, was given to Robert, the conqueror's eldest son; but they are entirely silent respecting the reason for such an appellation

being particularly applied to him. It could not
have arisen from his having introduced the custom of wearing short boots into this country, for
they were certainly in use among the Saxons long
before his birth: to hazard a conjecture of my
own, I should rather say he was the first among
the Normans who wore short boots, and derived
the cognomen by way of contempt, from his own
countrymen, for having so far complied with the
manners of the Anglo-Saxons. It was not long,
however, supposing this to be the case, before
his example was generally followed." The short
boots of the Normans appear at times to fit quite
close to the legs; in other instances they are
represented more loose and open; and though
the materials of which they were composed are
not particularized by ancient writers, we may rea-
sonably suppose them to have been made of leather; at least it is certain that about this time, a
sort of leathern boots, called bazans, were in
fashion; but they appear to have been chiefly
confined to the clergy.

"Among the various innovations," continues
Strutt, "made in dress by the Normans during
the twelfth century, none met with more marked
and more deserved disapprobation than that of
lengthening the toes of the shoes, and bringing

them forward to a sharp point. In the reign of Rufus, this custom was first introduced; and according to Orderic Vitalis, by a man who had distorted feet, in order to conceal his deformity;" but he adds, "the fashion was no sooner broached, than all those who were fond of novelty thought proper to follow it; and the shoes were made by the shoemakers in the form of a scorpion's tail." These shoes were called *pigaciæ*, and were adopted by persons of every class, both rich and poor. Soon after, a courtier, whose name was Robert, improved upon the first idea, by filling the vacant part of the shoe with tow, and twisting it round in the shape of a ram's horn; this ridiculous fashion excited much admiration. It was followed by the greater part of the nobility; and the author, for his happy invention, was honored with the cognomen *Cornardus*, or horned. The long pointed shoes were vehemently inveighed against by the clergy, and strictly forbidden to be worn by the religious orders. So far as we can judge from the drawings executed in the twelfth century, the fashion of wearing long-pointed shoes did not long maintain its ground. It was, however, afterward revived, and even carried to a more preposterous extent.

A specimen of the shoes that were worn at this

period, and which so excited the ire of the monk-
ish writers, is here given from the seal of Richard,

constable of Chester, in the reign of Stephen; in
the original the knight is on horseback, the stirrup
and spur are therefore seen in our cut.

The effigies of the early sovereigns of England, are generally represented in shoes decorated
with bands across, as if in imitation of sandals.
They are seldom colored black, as nearly all the
examples of earlier shoes in this country are. The
shoes of Henry II. are green, with bands of gold.
Those of Richard are also striped with gold; and
such richly decorated shoes became fashionable
among the nobility, and were generally worn by
royalty all over Europe. Thus, when the tomb of
Henry VI. of Sicily, who died in 1197, was opened
in the cathedral of Palermo, on the feet of the dead
monarch were discovered costly shoes, whose upper part was of cloth of gold, embroidered with
pearls, the sole being of cork, covered with the
same cloth of gold. These shoes reached to the
ankle, and were fastened with a little button in-

stead of a buckle. His queen, Constance, who
died in 1198, had upon her feet shoes also of cloth
of gold, which were fastened with leather straps
tied in knots, and on the upper part of them were
two openings, wrought with embroidery, which
showed that they had been once adorned with jewels. Boots ornamented with gold, and embroidered in elegant patterns, at this time became often
worn. King John of England, orders, in one instance, four pair of women's boots, one of them to
be embroidered with circles; and the effigy of the
succeeding monarch, Henry III., in Westminster
abbey, is chiefly remarkable for the splendor of the
boots he wears; they are crossed all over by gold-
en bands, thus forming a series of diamond-shaped
spaces, each one of which is filled with a figure of
a lion, the royal arms of England. One of these
splendid shoes is engraved in plate III., fig. 1.

   The shape of the sole of the shoes at this time,
may be seen from the cut here given of one found

in a tomb of the period, and called that of St.
Swithin, in Winchester cathedral. The shoe is
engraved in "Gough's Sepulchral Monuments,"

and the person who discovered it in the tomb thus
describes it: "The legs of the wearer were en-
closed in leathern boots or gaiters sewed with neatness, the thread was still to be seen. The soles
were small and round, rather worn, and of what
would be called an elegant shape at present; pointed at the toe and very narrow, and were made and
fitted to each foot. I have sent the pattern of one
of the soles, drawn by tracing it with a pencil from
the original itself, which I have in my possession."
Gough engraves the shoe of the natural size in his
work, the measurements being ten inches in length
from toe to heel, and three inches across the broad-
est part of the instep. It will be seen that they
are as perfectly "right and left," as any boots of
the present day; but as we have already shown,
this is a fashion of the most remote antiquity. As
these boots are at least as old as the time of John,
Shakspere's description in his dramatized history
of that sovereign, of the tailor, who eager to ac-
quaint his friend, the smith, of the prodigies the
skies had just exhibited, and whom Hubert saw

> " Standing in slippers which his nimble haste
> Had falsely thrust upon contrary feet,"

is strictly accurate: yet half a century ago, this
passage was adjudged to be one of the many proofs
of Shakspere's ignorance or carelessness. Dr.

Johnson, ignorant himself of the truth in this point, but yet, like all critics, determined to pass his verdict, makes himself supremely absurd, by saying in a note to this passage, with ridiculous solemnity, "Shakspere seems to have confounded the man's shoes with his gloves. He that is frighted or hurried may put his hand into the wrong glove, but either shoe will equally admit either foot. The author seems to be disturbed by the disorder which he describes."

In the "Art Union," a journal devoted to the fine arts, are a series of notices of the various forms of boots and shoes in Great Britain, by F. W. Fairholt, F. S. A., from which we may borrow the description of the elegant coverings for the feet in use in the reigns of the first three Edwards. Boots buttoned up the leg, or shoes buttoned up the centre, or secured like the Norman shoe in the second figures of the first cut given in this chapter, were common in the days of Edward I. and II. The splendid reign of the third Edward, says Mr. Fairholt, extending over half a century of national greatness, was remarkable for the variety and luxury, as well as the elegance of its costume; and this may be considered as the most glorious era in the annals of "the gentle craft," as the trade of shoemaking was anciently termed. Shoes and

4*

boots of the most sumptuous description are now
to be met with in contemporary paintings, sculptures, and illuminated manuscripts.   The boot and
shoe here engraved from the Arundel MS., No. 83,
executed about 1339 (pl. III., figs. 2 and 3), are fine
examples of the extent to which the tasteful ornament of these articles of dress was carried.   They
remind one of the boots "fretted with gold" and
embroidered in circles mentioned by John.   The
greatest variety of pattern and the richest contrasts
of color were aimed at by the maker and inventor
of shoes at this period, and with how happy an
effect the reader may judge, from the examples just
given, as well as from the three also engraved in
pl. III., Nos. 4, 5, and 6, and which are copied
from Smike's copies of the paintings, which formerly existed on the walls of St. Stephen's chapel at
Westminster, and which drawings now decorate
the walls of the meeting-room of the Society of
Antiquaries.   It is impossible to conceive any shoe
more exquisite in design than fig. 4, of our plate.
It is worn by a royal personage, and it brings for-
cibly to mind the rose windows, and other details
of the architecture of this period; but for beauty
of pattern and splendor of effect this English shoe
of the middle ages is "beyond all Greek, beyond
all Roman fame," for their sandals and shoes have

not half "the glory of regality contained in this one specimen." The fifth figure in the same plate is simpler in design but not less striking in effect, being colored (as the previous one is) solid black, the red hose adding considerably to its effect. No. 6, is still more peculiar, and is cut all over into a geometric pattern, and with a fondness for quaint display in dress peculiar to those times, the left shoe is black and the stocking blue, the other leg of the same figure being clothed in a black stocking and a white shoe. The form of this latter one is that usually worn by persons of all classes, of course omitting the elaborate ornament. The shoe was cut very low over the instep, the heel being entirely covered, and a band fastened by a small buckle or button passing round the ankle secured it to the foot.

The boots and shoes worn during the fourteenth century, were of peculiar form, and the toes which were lengthened to a point, turned inward or outward according to the taste of the wearer. In the reign of Richard II., they became immensely long, so that it was asserted they were chained to the knee of the wearer, in order to allow him to walk about with ease and freedom. It was of course only the nobility who could thus inconvenience themselves, and it might have been adopted by

them as a distinction; still very pointed toes were
worn by all who could afford to be fashionable.
The cut here given exhibits the sole of a shoe of
this period, from an actual specimen in the posses-

sion of C. Roach Smith, F. S. A., and was discovered in the neighborhood of Whitefriars, in digging
deep under ground into what must have originally
been a receptable for rubbish, among which these
old shoes had been thrown, and they are probably
the only things of the kind now in existence.

Two specimens of boots of the time of Edward
IV., are here given to show their general form at
that period. The first is copied from the Royal
MS., No. 15, E. 6, and is of black leather, with a

long upturned toe; the top of the boot is of lighter
leather, and thus it bears a resemblance to the top-
boots of a later age, of which it may be considered
as the prototype.   The other boot, from a print
dated 1515, is more curious; the top of the boot is
turned down, and the entire centre opens from the
top, to the instep, and is drawn together by laces
or ties across the leg, so that it bears considerable
resemblance in this point to the Cothurnus of the
ancients.

Fashion ran at this time from one extreme to the
other, and the shoes which were at one time so
long at the toe as to be inconvenient, now became as absurdly broad, and it was made the subject of sumptuary laws to restrain both extremes.
Thus Edward IV. enacted that any shoemaker who
made for unprivileged persons (the nobility being
exempted) any shoes or boots, the toes of which
exceeded two inches in length, should forfeit twenty shillings, one noble to be paid to the king, another to the cordwainers of London, and the third
to the chamber of London.   This only had the
effect of widening the toes ; and Paradin says that
they were then so very broad as to exceed the
measure of a good foot.   This continued until the
reign of Mary, who, by a proclamation, prohibited
their being worn wider at the toe than six inches.

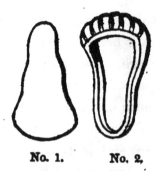

No. 1.   No. 2.

We have here engraved two specimens of these
broad-toed shoes of the time of Henry VIII. No. 1
is copied from the monumental effigy of Katharine,
the wife of Sir Thomas Babynton, who died 1543,
and is buried in Morley church, near Derby. It is
an excellent specimen of the sort of sole preferred
by the fashionables of that day. The second cut
exhibits a front view of a similarly-made shoe.
They were formed of leather, but generally the
better classes wore them of rich velvet and silk,
the various colors of which were exhibited in slashes at the toes, which were most sparingly covered
by the velvet of which the shoe was composed. In
the curious full-length portrait of the poetical Earl
of Surrey, at Hampton Court, he is represented in
shoes of red velvet, having bands of a darker tint
placed across them diagonally; which bands are
decorated with a row of gold ornaments.

During the reign of Edward VI., a sort of shoe

with a pointed toe was worn, not unlike the modern one. It was of velvet, generally, with the upper classes ; of leather, with the poorer ones. The former indulged in a series of slashes over the upper leather, which the others had not. We give here two specimens of these shoes, from prints

dated 1577 and 1588 ; and they will serve to show the sort of form adopted, as well as the varied way in which the slashes of the velvet appeared, and which altered with the wearer's taste. Philip Stubbes, the puritanical author of the " Anatomy of Abuses," 1588, declares that the fashionables then wore " corked shoes, puisnets, pantoffles, and slippers, some of them of black velvet, some of white, some of green, and some of yellow ; some of Spanish leather, and some of English, stitched with silk and embroidered with gold and silver all over the foot with gewgaws innumerable." Rich and expensive shoe-ties were now brought into use, and large sums were lavished upon their decorations.

John Taylor, the water poet, alludes to the extravagance of those who

"Wear a farm in shoe-strings edged with gold,
And spangled garters worth a copy-hold."

The shoe-roses were made of lace, which was as beautiful, costly, and elaborate, as that which composed the ruff for the neck, or ruffles for the wrist. They were elaborately decorated with needlework and gold and silver thread.

During the reign of the first Charles, the boots (which were made of fine Spanish leather, and were of a buff color) became very large and wide at the top. Indeed, they were so wide at times, as to oblige the wearer to stride much in walking, a habit that was much ridiculed by the satirists of the day. There was a print published during this reign of a dandy in the height of fashion whose legs are " incased in boot-hose tops tied about the middle of the calf, as long as a pair of shirt-sleeves, double at the end like a ruff-band : the top of his boots very large, fringed with lace, and turned down as low as his spurs, which jingled like the bells of a morris-dancer as he walked." These boots were made very long in the toe, thus, of this exquisite we are told, " the feet of his boots were two inches too long."

The boot-tops at this time were made wide, and

were capable of being turned over beneath the knee, which they completely covered when they were uplifted.   They were of course made of pliant leather to allow of this—"Spanish leather," according to Ben Jonson.

During the whole of the Commonwealth large boot-tops of this kind were worn even by the puritans ; they were, however, large only, and not decorated with costly lace.   The shoes worn were generally particularly simple in their construction and form, and those who did not wish to be classed among the vain and frivolous, took care to have their toes sharp at the point, as a distinction between themselves and the "graceless gallants," who generally wore theirs very broad.

With the restoration of Charles II. came the large French boot, in which the courtiers of "Louis le grand," always delighted to exhibit their legs. Of the amplitude of its tops, the woodcut will give

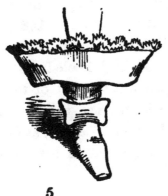

5

an idea, it is copied from one worn by a courtier of
Charles's train, in the engravings illustrative of his
coronation. The boot is decorated with lace all
round the upper part, and that portion of the leg
which the boot encases, seems fitted easily with
pliant leather: over the instep is a broad band of
the same material, beneath which the spur was fastened; and the heel is high, and toe broad, of all
the boots and shoes then fashionable.

A boot of the end of this reign, forms fig. 7, of
our third plate, and is copied from a pair which
hang up in Shottesbrooke church, Berkshire, above
a tomb, in accordance with the old custom, of bury-
ing a knight with his martial equipments over his
grave, originally consisting of his shield, sword,
gloves, and spurs, the boots being a later and more
absurd introduction. The pair which we are now
describing, are formed of fine buff leather, the tops
are red, and so are the heels, which are very high,
the toes being cut exceedingly square.

With the great revolution of 1688, and his majesty William III., came in the large jack-boot, and
the high-quartered, high-heeled, and buckled shoe,
which only expired at the end of the last century.
Sir Samuel Rush Meyrick, has one of these jack-
boots in his collection of armor, at Goodrich court;
and it has been engraved in his work on ancient

arms and armor, from which it is copied in plate
III., fig. 8. It is a remarkably fine specimen of
these inconvenient things, and is as straight and
stiff and formal, as the most inveterate Dutchman
could wish. The heel it will be perceived is very
high, and the press upon the instep very great, and
consequently injurious to the foot, and altogether
detrimental to comfort. An immense piece of
leather covers the instep, through which the spur
is affixed, and to the back of the boot, just above
the heel, is appended an iron rest for the spur.
Such were the boots of the English cavalry and
infantry, and in such cumbrous articles did they
fight in the low countries, following the example of
Charles XII., of Sweden, whose figure has become
so identified with them, that the imagination can
not easily separate the sovereign from the boots in
which he is so constantly painted, and of which a
specimen may be seen in his full-length portrait,
preserved in the British museum.

A boot was worn by civilians, less rigid than the
one last described, the leg taking more of the natural shape, and the tops being smaller, of a more
pliant kind, and sometimes slightly ornamented
round the edges.

We have here two examples of ladies' shoes, as
worn during the period of which we are discussing.

The first figure, copied from volume 67, of the
"Gentleman's Magazine," shows the peculiar
shape of the shoe, as well as the clog beneath;
these clogs were merely single pieces of stout

leather, which were fastened beneath the heel and
instep, and appear to be only extra hinderances in
walking, which must materially have destroyed any
little pliancy which the original shoe would have
allowed the foot to retain.   The second figure is
copied from the first volume of "Hone's Every
Day Book," and that author says, "This was the
fashion that beautified the feet of the fair, in the
reign of King William and Queen Mary."
Holme, in his "Academy of Armory," is minutely
diffuse on the gentle craft: he engraves the form of
a pair of wedges, which he says "is to raise up a
shoe in the instep, when it it is too straight for the
top of the foot;" and thus compassionates ladies'
sufferings: "Shoemakers love to put ladies in
their stocks, but these wedges, like merciful justi-
ces, upon complaint, soon do ease and deliver them.
If the eye turns to the cut—to the cut of the sole,

Pl. 3.

with the line of beauty adapted by the cunning
of the workman's skill, to stilt the female foot: if
the reader behold that association, let wonder
cease, that a venerable master in coat armor,
should bend his quarterings to the quarterings of a
lady's shoe, and forgetful of heraldic forms, conde-
scend from his high estate to use similitudes."

This shape, once firmly established, was the
prevailing one during the reigns of George I. and
II. Figs. 9, 10, 11, 12, 13, of plate III., will fully display the different forms and style, adopted by the
fashionables of that day. They always wore red
heels, at least all persons who pretended to gentil-
ity. The fronts of the gentlemen's shoes were
very high, and on gala-days or showy occasions, a
buff shoe was worn. The ladies appear to have
preferred silk or velvet to leather: thus fig. 10 is
entirely made of a figured blue silk, and it has
bright red heels and silver buckles. Fig. 11 is of
brown leather, with a red heel, and a red rose for
a tie above the instep. Fig. 12 is altogether red,
in a pattern of different strengths of tint; the tie
and heels being deepest in color.

Her majesty's grand bal costumé, given during
the past year, revived for a night the fashion of a
century ago: and the author of these pages, was
then under the necessity of hunting up the few re-

maining makers of wooden heels, in order to furnish the correct shoe, to complete the costume of many of the most distinguished individuals, who figured on that occasion.

The making of the high-heeled shoe, was at all times a matter of great judgment and nicety of operation; the position required to be given to the heel, the aptitude of the eye and hand, necessary to the cutting down of the wood; the sewing in of the cover, kid, stuff, silk, or satin, as it might be: the getting in and securing the wood or "block;" the bracing the cover round the block; and the beautifully defined stitching, which went from corner to corner, all round the heel part, demanding altogether the cleverness of first-rate ability.

The shoes became lower in the quarters during the reign of George III., and the heel was made less clumsy. As fashion varied, larger or smaller buckles were used, and the heel was thrust further beneath the foot until about 1780, when the shoe

took the form here delineated, and which is copied from Mr. Fairholt's notes in the "Art Union," already alluded to.

From the same source, we borrow the following notices by the same writer: "About 1790, a change in the fashion of ladies' shoes occurred. They were made very flat and low in the heel, in reality more like a slipper than a shoe. This engraving, copied from a real specimen, will show

the peculiarity of its make: the low quarters, the diminutive heel, and the plaited riband and small tie in front, in place of the buckle which began to be occasionally discontinued. The duchess of York, at this time, was remarkable for the smallness of her foot, and a colored print of 'the exact size of the duchess' shoe,' was published by Fores, in 1791. It measures five and three quarters inches in length; the breadth of the sole being only one and three quarters inches. It is made of green silk, ornamented with gold stars; is bound with scarlet silk; the heel is scarlet, and the shape is similar to the one engraved above, except that the heel is exactly in the modern style." Models of this fairy shoe were made of china, as ornaments for the chimney, or drawing-room table, with cupids hovering around it.

Shoes of the old fashion, with high heels and

buckles, appear in prints of the early part of 1800; but buckles became unfashionable, and shoe-strings eventually triumphed, although less costly and elegant in their construction. The prince of Wales was petitioned by the alarmed buckle-makers, to discard his new-fashioned strings, and take again to buckles, by way of bolstering up their trade; but the fate of these articles was sealed, and the prince's good-natured compliance with their wishes, did little to prevent their downfall. The buckles worn at the end of 1700, were generally exceedingly small, and so continued until they were finally disused.

Early in the reign of George III., the close fitting gentleman's boot became general; the material used for the leg was termed *grain-leather*, the flesh side being left brown, and the grain blackened, and kept to the sight. In currying this sort of leather for the boot-leg, it went, in the lower part, through an ingenious process of contraction, to give it *life;* so that the heel of the wearer might go into it and come out again the easier; the boot, at the same time, when on, catching snugly round the small of the leg, in a sort of stocking fit.

After this appeared the "Hessian," a boot worn over the tight-fitting pantaloon, the uppeaking front bearing a silk tassel. This boot was introduced from Germany, about 1789, and sometimes was called the Austrian boot. Rees, in his "Art and Mystery of the Cordwainer," published in 1813, says, "The form at first was odious, as the close boot was then in wear, but like many fashions, at first frightful, it was then pitied, and at last adopted."

The top-boot was worn early in the reign of George III., and took the fulness of the Hessian in its lower part, and on the introduction of the "Wellington," the same fulness was retained.

To describe the last-named boot were useless, it has become, *par excellence*, the common boot, and is perhaps as universally known as the fame of the distinguished hero WELLINGTON.

CHAPTER III.

UPON critically examining the various forms
assumed by the coverings for the feet adopted
by the nations around us, we shall find that they
were in no small degree modified by the circumstances with which they were surrounded, or the
necessities of the climate they inhabited.

Thus the northern nations enswathed their legs
in skins, and used the same material for the shoes,
binding the whole in warm folds about the leg,
the thongs being fastened to them in the manner
represented in plate IV., fig. 1, and which is
copied from a full length figure of a Russian boor,
in 1768. The sandal of a Russian lady of the
same period, is given in the same plate, fig. 2,
and the men of Friesland at the same time, wore
sandals or shoes of a similar construction, the
common people generally wearing a close leathern
shoe and clog, something like those in use in the

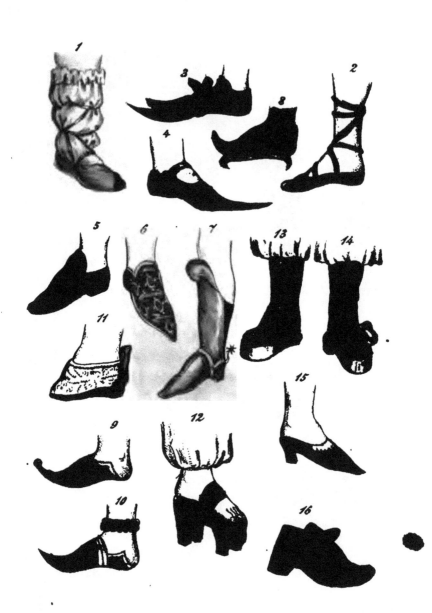

Pl. 4.

middle ages, one delineated in fig. 3 of our plate, and is represented on the feet of a countrywoman, in the curious series of costumes of Finland, engraved in "Jeffery's Collection of the Dresses of different Nations," published in 1757, and which were copied from some very rare prints, at least a century earlier in point of date. Another female's shoe is given in fig. 4; it is a low slipper-like shoe, and is secured by a band across the instep, having an ornamental clasp, like a brooch, to secure it on each side of the foot; it was probably a coarsely-made piece of jewelry, with glass or cheap stones set around it; as the people of this country at that time were fond of such showy decorations, and particularly upon their shoes. The noblemen and ladies always decorated theirs with ornaments and jewels all over the upper surface, of which we give two specimens in figs. 5 and 6: the former upon the foot of a nobleman, the latter upon that of a matron of the upper classes. It will be seen, that both are very elegant, and must have been very showy wear.

The boots of an Hungarian gentleman, in 1700, may be seen in fig. 7, of plate IV., and such boots were common to Bohemia at the same period. They are chiefly remarkable for the way in which they are cut upward from the middle

of the thigh to the knee, and then curl over in front
of the leg.

A Tartarian lady of 1577, is exhibited by John
Wiegel, the engraver of Nuremburgh, in his work
on dress, in the boots delineated in fig. 8. They
are remarkable for the sole to which they are affixed, and which was, no doubt, formed of some
strong substance, probably with metallic hooks to
assist the wearer in walking a mountainous country
where frosts abound.

Descending toward the south, we shall find a
lighter sort of shoe in use, and one partaking more
of the character of a slipper, used more as a protection for the sole of the foot in walking, than as
an article of warmth. Thus the shoes generally
used in the East, scarcely do more than cover the
toes, yet, from constant use, the natives hardly ever
allow them to slip from the feet. The learned author of the notes to "Knight's Pictorial Bible,"
speaking from personal observation of these articles, says, "The common shoe in Turkey or Arabia
is like our slipper *with* quarters, except that it has
a sharp and prolonged toe turned up." No shoes
in western Asia have ears, and they are generally
of colored leather—red or yellow morocco in Turkey and Arabia, and green shagreen in Persia. In
the latter country, the shoe or slipper in general

use (having no quarters), has a very high heel; but with this exception, the heels in these countries are generally flat. No shoes or even boots have more than a single sole (like what we call "pumps"), which in wet weather imbibes the water freely. When the shoe without quarters is used, a slipper, with quarters, but without a sole, is worn inside, and the outer one alone is thrown off on entering a house. But in Persia, instead of this inner shoe of leather, they use a worsted sock. Those shoes that have quarters are usually worn without any inner covering for the foot. The peasantry and the nomade tribes usually go barefoot, or wear a rude sandal or shoe of their own manufacture; those who possess a pair of red leather or other shoes, seldom wear them except on holyday occasions, so that they last a long time, if not so long as among the Maltese, with whom a pair of shoes endures for several generations, being, even on holyday occasions, more frequently carried in the hand than worn on the feet. The boots are generally of the same construction and material as the shoes; and the general form may be compared to that of the buskin, the neight varying from the mid-leg to near the knee. They are of capacious breadth, except among the Persians whose boots generally fit close to the leg, and are mostly of a

sort of Russia leather, uncolored; whereas those of
other people are, like the slipper, of red and yellow morocco.   There is also a boot or shoe for
walking in frosty weather, which differs from the
common one only in having under the heel iron
tips, which, being partly bent vertically with a jag-
ged edge, give a hold on the ice, which prevents
slipping, and are particularly useful in ascending
or descending the frozen mountain paths — remind-
ing us of the sort of boot worn by Tartarian ladies, as
given in fig. 8.   The shoes of the oriental ladies
are sometimes highly ornamented; the covering
part being wrought with gold, silver, and silk, and
perhaps set with jewels, real or imitated.   Examples of such decorated shoes are given in plate
IV., figs. 9 and 10, and will sufficiently explain
themselves to the eye of the reader, rendering detailed description unnecessary.   The shoes of noblemen are of precisely similar construction.

In China, the boots and shoes of the men are
worn as clumsy and inelegant as in any country.

They are broad at the toe, and sometimes up-turned. We give a specimen of both in the fore-going engraving. They are no doubt easy to wear.

Not so are the ladies' shoes, for they only are al-lowed the privilege of discomfort, fashion having in this country declared in favor of small feet, and the prejudice of the people having gone with it, the feet of all ladies of decent rank in society, are cramped in early life, by being placed in so strait a confinement, that their growth is retarded, and they are not more than three or four inches in length, from the toe to the heel. By the smallness of the foot the rank or high-breeding of the lady is decided on, and the utmost torment is endured by the girls in early life, to insure themselves this dis-tinction in rank; the lower classes of females not being allowed to torture themselves in the same manner. The Chinese poets frequently indulge in panegyrics on the beauty of these crippled mem-bers of the body, and none of their heroines are considered perfect without excessively small feet, when they are affectionately termed by them "the little golden lilies." It is needless to say that the tortures of early youth are succeeded by a crip-pled maturity, a Chinese lady of high birth being scarcely able to walk without assistance. A speci-men of such a foot and shoe is given in plate III.,

fig. 11. These shoes are generally made of silk
and embroidered in the most beautiful manner, with
flowers and ornaments, in colored silk and threads
of gold and silver. A piece of stout silk is generally attached to the heel for the convenience of
pulling up the shoe.

Having bestowed some attention on ancient
Egypt, we may briefly allude to the shoes of modern times, as given in Lane's work devoted to the
history of the manners and customs of the modern
Egyptians. They, like the Persian ones, have an
upturned toe, and may with equal ease be drawn
on and thrown off. Yet a shoe is also worn with a
high instep and high in the heel, which will be
best understood by the first figure in the accompanying cut.

The Turkish ladies of the sixteenth century, and
very probably much earlier, wore a very high shoe
known in Europe by the name of a "chopine."
In the voyages and travels of N. de Nicholay Dau-
phinoys, Seigneur D'Arfreville, valet de chambre
and geographer to the king of France, printed at
Lyons, 1568, one of the ladies of the grand seign-

eur's seraglio, is represented in a pair of chopines, of which we copy one in plate III., fig. 12. This fashion spread in Europe in the early part of the seventeenth century, and it is alluded to by Hamlet, in act ii., scene 2, when he exclaims, "Your ladyship is nearer heaven than when I saw you last, by the altitude of a chopine," by which it appears that something of the kind was known in England, where it may have been introduced from Venice, as the ladies there wore them of the most exaggerated size. Coryat, in his "Crudities," 1611, says: "There is one thing used of the Venetian women, and some others dwelling in the cities and towns subject to signiory of Venice, that is not to be observed (I think) among any other women in Christendom"—the reader must remember that it was new to Coryat, but a common fashion in the East—"which is so common in Venice that no woman whatsoever goeth without it, either in her house or abroad—a thing made of wood and covered with leather of sundry colors; some with white, some red, some yellow. It is called a *chapiney*, which they never wear under their shoes. Many of these are curious painted; some of them I have also seen fairly gilt; so uncomely a thing, in my opinion, that it is a pity this foolish custom is not clean banished and exterminated out of the city. There

6*

are many of these chapineys of a great height
even half a yard high, which maketh many of their
women, that are very short, seem much taller than
the tallest women we have in England. Also, I
have heard it observed among them, that by how
much the nobler a woman is, by so much the higher
are her chapineys. All their gentlewomen, and
most of their wives and widows that are of any
wealth, are assisted and supported either by men
or women, when they walk abroad, to the end they
might not fall. They are borne up most commonly
by the left arm; otherwise they might quickly take
a fall." In Douce's Illustrations of Shakspere, a
woodcut of such a chapiney, or chopine, is given,
which is here copied; and it is an excellent ex-

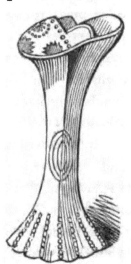

ample of the thing, showing the decoration which was at times bestowed on it.

Douce quotes some curious particulars of this fashion, in "Raymond's Voyage through Italy," 1648, and the following curious account of the chopine occurs: " This place [Venice] is much frequented by the walking may-poles: I mean the women. They wear their coats half too long for their bodies, being mounted on their *chippeens* (which are as high as a man's leg); they walke betweene two handmaids, majestically deliberating of every step they take." Howel also says of the Venetian women: "They are low and of small stature for the most part, which makes them to raise their bodies upon high shoes, called *chapins*, which gave me occasion to say that the Venetian ladies were made of three things, one part of them was wood, meaning their chapins, another part was their apparel, and the third part was a woman. The senate hath often endeavored to take away the wearing of those high shoes, but all women are so passionately delighted with this kind of state, that no law can wean them from it." Douce adds, that "some have supposed that the jealousy of Italian husbands gave rise to the invention of the chopine;" and quotes a story from a French author, . to show their dislike to an alteration; he also says,

that "the first ladies who rejected the use of the
chopine, were the daughters of the doge Domin-
ico Contareno, about the year 1670." The chopine, or some kind of high shoe, was occasionally
used in England. Bulwer, in his "Artificial
Changeling," p. 550, complains of this fashion as
a monstrous affectation, and says that his country-
women therein imitated the Venetian and Persian
ladies. In "Sandy's Travels," 1615, there is a figure of a Turkish lady·with chopines, and it is not
improbable that the Venetians might have bor-
rowed them from the Greek islands in the Archipelago. We know that something similar was in
use among the ancient Greeks. Xenophon, in
Œconomics, mentions the wife of Ischomachus as
wearing high shoes, for increasing her stature.
They are still worn by the women in many parts
of Turkey, but more particularly at Aleppo.
Douce's notice of their antiquity, is curiously cor-
roborated by the discovery in the tombs of ancient
Egypt of such shoes. They are formed of a stout
sole of wood, to which is affixed four round props,
raising the wearer a foot in height; specimens were
among the collections of Mr. Salt, the British con-
sul in Egypt, from which some of the choicest
Egyptian antiquities in the national collection were
obtained. The other remark of Douce's, that they

were probably derived from the Greek islands of
the Archipelago, is confirmed by the fact that high-
soled boots and shoes were much coveted by the ladies there, to raise their stature, and were worn
when chopines had long been disused; thus the
high-soled boots delineated in plate IV., fig. 13, are
found upon the feet of "a young lady of Argenti-
era," one of these islands, in a print dated 1700;
and, in another of the same date, giving the costume of a lady of the neighboring island of Naxos,
the shoe shown in fig. 14, is worn.

Of the modern European nations with whom we
have been most in contact—Spain, France, and the
Netherlands—their boots and shoes have so nearly
resembled our own, as to render a detailed description scarcely necessary. Indeed, as France has
been tacitly submitted to as the *arbiter elegantia-
rum* in all matters of dress, much has been derived
thence.

There was, however, a French shoe that we do
not ever appear to have adopted; it was made low
in the quarters and ended at the instep; there was
no covering for the heel, or the sides of the foot
beyond it. The fashion spread to Venice, and the
figure of a Venetian lady of 1750, has supplied us
with the specimen in plate IV., fig. 15.

The *sabots* of France, is another peculiarity

which we never adopted, and which our peasantry
have always looked on with great distaste; and it
became popularly said of William III., that he had
saved us from popery, slavery, and *wooden shoes*.
They are generally clumsy enough; their large
size, and bad fit, are generally improved by the introduction of others made of list, which give
warmth and steadiness to the foot. A small wood-
en shoe is, however, made in Normandy, and else
where, much like that which came into fashion
about 1790, with an imitation of its fringes and
pointed toe, and which is generally painted black;
the ordinary *sabot* being totally unadorned, and the
color of the wood. In the cut here given, both are
introduced. Fig. 1, is the ordinary shoe; fig. 2,
the extraordinary or genteel one.

Fig. 1.   Fig. 2.

And now, having in the pursuit of our history of
boots and shoes,

" Travelled the wide world all over,"

let us not dismiss the subject, without a parting
glance at the sister island, and look at the

"brogues" of Ireland; which upon the authority of Mr. and Mrs. S. C. Hall, especially deserve our attention. In their work on Ireland, they engrave the figure of this article, which we copy, plate IV., fig. 16, and say: "The brogue, or shoe, of the Irish peasantry, differs in its construction from the shoe of any other country. It was formerly made of untanned hide, but, for the last century at least, it has been made of tanned leather. The leather of the uppers is much stronger than what is used in the strongest shoes; being made of cowhide dressed for the purpose, and it never had an inside lining, like the ordinary shoe; the sole leather is generally of an inferior description. The process of making the brogue, is certainly different from that of shoemaking; and the tools used in the work, except the hammer, pinchers, and knife, bear little analogy. The awl, though used in common by those operators, is much larger than the largest used by the shoemaker, and unlike in the bend and form. The regular brogue was of two sorts, the single and double pump, the former consisted of the sole and uppers only; the latter had a welt sewed between the sole and upper leather, which gave it a stouter appearance and stronger consistency; in modern times, the broguemaker has assimilated his manufacture to the shoe, by sewing the

welt on an inner sole, and then attaching the outer
sole to it, in shoe-fashion. In the process of making the regular brogue, there formerly were neither hemp, wax, nor bristles, used by the workmen,
the sewing all being performed with a thong, made
of horsehide, prepared for the purpose." Thus
the construction of this article is quite different from
that of the English shoe; and it is made and
stitched without a last, the upper leather and side
being secured by sewing together; it is then
turned inside out, and for the first time put upon
the last, and being well-fitted to it by a smooth iron
surface, it is placed before the fire to dry and hard-
en. "The heel of the brogue is made of what
they call 'jumps,' tanner's shavings stuck together with a kind of paste, and pressed hard, and
dried, either before the fire or in the sun. This,
when properly dried, is cut to the size of the
heel, and sewed down with the thong, and then
covered with a top-piece of very thin sole-leather,
fastened on with deal or sally pegs; and in this
one particular they had to boast over the shoemakers, in the neatness of execution. When the
brogue is ready to be taken off the last, they
give it the last finish by rubbing it over with a
woollen rag saturated in tallow, and then the
brogue is considered fit for sale. The brogue is

worn larger than the foot, and the space is filled
up with a sap of hay or straw. They are considered by the country people more durable for
field-labor, being less liable to rip in the sewing,
than if put together with hemp and wax; and
being cheaper than shoes, are in more general
use, although there are few people, particularly
females, who can afford it, who do not keep
shoes for Sunday or holyday wear. The brogue-
makers pride themselves in the antiquity of their
trade; and boast over the shoemakers, whom they
consider a spurious graft on their most noble art."

Sir Walter Scott, in his "Minstrelsy of the Scot-
tish Border," has noticed a peculiarity in the make
of the "original" shoe of that country, in the notes
to the ballad of the "Souters," or shoemakers of
Selkirk, who achieved immortality in song, by their
bravery in aiding their sovereign, James IV.; in
the fatal field of Flodden; he says "the single-
soled shoon," made by the souters of Selkirk, were
a sort of brogues, with a single thin sole; the purchaser himself performing the further operation of
sewing on another of thick leather. The rude and
imperfect state of this manufacture, sufficiently
evinces the antiquity of the craft. He notices "a
singular custom observed at conferring the freedom
of the burgh. Four or five bristles, such as are

used by shoemakers, are attached to the seal of the
burgess ticket. The new-made burgess must dip
in his wine, and pass through his mouth, in token
of respect for the souters of Selkirk. This cere-
mony is on no account dispensed with." And
when Sir Walter afterward adds, in a note that *he*
has "himself the honor to be a souter of Selkirk,"
we may feel the additional zest that would give to
the chorus of their old trade-song :—

> "Up wi' the souters of Selkirk,
> And down wi' the Earl of Home ;
> And up wi' a' the braw lads,
> That sew the single-soled shoon."

CHAPTER IV.

AT what period of the world the trade in question became a separate means of obtaining a livelihood, it is now impossible to say. At first no doubt, every one made their own shoes; the mere wrapping up of the foot in a piece of flexible skin being matter of little difficulty, but according to Rosseline, whom we quoted in a former chapter, shoemakers' shops existed in Egypt at a very early period.

That it became, however, in a very early age, a trade, we may infer from the fact of it being an injunction of the Jewish social system, that every one, no matter what his rank or wealth, should be compelled to acquire the means of self-support by an acquaintance with some art or other, the better to secure himself against the adverse vicissitudes of life. (See note on Mark vi. 3, in Pictorial Bible, vol. 3.) This obligation naturally affords reason for belief in a variety of professions; and the shoe, from its constant requisition, may, therefore, be supposed to have given rise to one of the earliest.

In one of the Greek dramatic writings, allusion is made to the daily earnings of the shoemaker; and in the far-famed anecdote of Apelles exposing to public scrutiny some masterpiece of his painting, the criticism of the cobbler, about the form or disposition of the latchet or tie of the shoe, implies, as in the other case, a distinctive character in the calling : the one receives his daily wages as a regular acknowledged workman; and the other, from his proficiency in his art, detects at once an error in the imitation.

The streets of Rome in the reign of Domitian, as Fosbrooke tells us in his " Dictionary of Antiquities," were at one time so filled with cobblers' stalls, (*cobbler* being the usual way among writers of naming the profession), that the emperor had to issue an order to clear them away, probably to some less ambitious situation—to the narrow and by-places of the city.   St. Anianus, a contemporary with St. Mark, as Alban Butler writes in his Lives of the Saints, was a shoemaker; and Crispin and Crispianus, brothers and martyrs, have the well-known repute of belonging to the trade ; they are its patrons, and have their fête-days yet in

all catholic countries; and though there is no longer any religious observance of the day in England,
the name of Crispin is still placed in the church
calendar against the 25th of October : and the shoemaker has still his traditions and his usages connected with the time.

The law of England formerly, not only took cog-
nizance of the quality of the leather which the
shoemaker wrought into his goods, but of the number of stitches that he furnished. In one of the
small towns in the north of England, the custom
of gauging shoes brought to market was prevalent
until lately, and the gauger had legal authority to
take away any shoe which had not the proper number of stitches. As his measure he used the breadth
of his thumb, which was meant for an inch. This,
therefore, is not an unpleasant retrospection; the
king and his parliament making enactments concerning the quality of the leather and scrutinizing
even the number of stitches.

The trade, as at present conducted in London
and other large towns, may be divided into two
departments, viz.: the bespoke and the ready-
made, or sale-trade. The first of these ranks as
chief, on account of the superiority of the article;
although the latter is the most general, and is pat-
ronized by the bulk of the population.

A lady or gentleman requiring boots or shoes, pays a visit to a respectable shop, and the measure is taken, either by the master or the clicker; the order is entered in the order-book, and the time named when they are to be ready. After the departure of the customer, the first business is to select a pair of lasts adapted to the feet—the measure is then applied to the length and circumference, and if suitable in the general form and proportions, the number of the last entered in a column opposite the name, &c.

The next business is to cut the pattern in paper; and, presuming it to be a lady's boot, the greatest care is taken in seeing that it stands well—neither dropping back, nor pitching too much forward. The goloshes round the side, the leather toe-caps, or whatever the form may be, of the lower part of the boot, has its pattern cut also in paper; for much depends on the correctness of these little matters.

The linen linings are then cut true to this pattern; the cashmere, prunella, or cloth, cut to form the outside, and the morocco, patent leather, or cordovan, added for the goloshing; and in this state it is given to the binder. Great care is now required and exacted, in working up the boot-leg true to the pattern; and if it be lace, button, or elastic, the binder has it in her power to spoil the whole affair. More, perhaps, depends on fitting the work, than the workmanship; a union, therefore, of skill, in these two points, constitutes a good boot-binder. The leg is next passed on to the *closer*, who, with the awl, instead of the needle, closes the seams of the golosh; and then, having lasted the boot, attaches the leather by means of a neat row of stabbing round the edge, thoroughly through the leg and its lining. This is the most secure, the neatest, and also the most expensive method, of getting up a good boot-leg.

This boot-leg, which has been twice sent out from the shop, now comes in to be again handed over to the maker, who receives the lasts, together with the leather soles, insoles, welts, stiffenings, shank-pieces, and other little matters essential to the work; not omitting, if the master knows his business, or considers the comfort of his customers, a good piece of *felt*, to insert *between* the insole and outsole, to prevent the intolerable nuisance of creaking. Neglect this, and besides the music (the fillings, which are bits of leather pasted between the soles, and which the workman is obliged to put in to make a level sole), you get lumps, after a little wear, at the bottom of the tread, which give great pain, and often produce corns and callosities on the soles of the feet.

It would be tedious to the reader to describe the various manipulations of the workman in making a pair of boots. If he accomplishes his work in the course of a day, he does well; and keeping the boots on the last during the night, to dry and get solid, is all that is required of him before bringing them to the shop.

If he has attended to all his instructions for width of tread, thickness of forepart, thinness of waist, height of heel, left no pegs sticking up, and kept his work clean, there is every probability of the lady being pleased, the master pleased, clicker pleased, workman pleased. But should either have failed, inadvertently or through carelessness, in one of the minute matters before mentioned, the boots are returned, and the whole must be gone over again.

Few ladies are aware of the many little points required to produce a good article with precision of fit; but let them consider, before they try another *artiste*, that the first failure may insure a correct fit the second time, and give no further trouble to them perhaps for life. A little patience at the proper time, would often save a world of annoyance in running from one shop to another, only to find out that all were pretty much alike.

In describing the other department, and by far

the most general in large towns, the ready-made trade, it may at first be supposed that all the evils of the bespoke system may be avoided. According to Barny O'Rierdon, in Ireland they are entirely avoided, as a man comes into market with a bar-row full of brogues, and every one helps himself; there is no measuring in the case, and if a brogue is too long, he claps a wisp of straw in the toe.

There is a large class of persons in London, &c., who sell boots and shoes, but do not manufacture them. The greater part of those persons know no more how a boot or shoe is made, than the boots and shoes can be said to possess such knowledge. These articles are principally made in the country, or the eastern part of the metropolis, and sent up for sale. Perhaps a hundred dozen pairs are made on one pair of lasts; the makers, of course, have no idea who will be the purchasers, or of the form of the feet of the parties who may wear them; nor do they care, their object being merely the sale and the money.

Persons may occasionally purchase a pair of these articles which will suit them tolerably well, as there is no rule without an exception; but for one such instance, there are, perhaps, fifty to the contrary. While some may prove good, others will be, perhaps, worthless; and though some persons

may be satisfied, most people will have abundant
cause to regret having risked a purchase.

In the *"cheap women's trade,"* there is also much
deception practised; so that *cheap* is only another
word for what at last proves to be, perhaps, the
dearest part of the female's expenditure for wearing apparel.

The cause of the evil here indicated must be
ascribed to one of those many misconceptions of
people's own affairs, which are so often made manifest in the conduct of individuals and classes.
Masters and workmen, quarrelling with each other,
do not see, in the blinded and blinding system of
their reprisals, what must finally be the result.
The employer, in some cases, must be ignorant of
the effect of his curtailments; and the journeyman
as ignorant as to the method he takes to protect
himself against such injustice. It is thus that the
woman's shoemaker, more than any other class in
the trade, has found himself lowered within the
last twenty-five or thirty years, in the scale of society; and his abilities also, as a workman, deterio-
rated; the master at the same time losing his own
proper position, through the inferiority of those
articles he sells, and the public in general, as well
as the character of the nation itself, in a sense,
injured. The master curtails, or the journeyman

exacts too much, differences ensue, fresh men are
employed, and the old ones, finding they must do
something for a living, move about and struggle on
as they can, and ultimately, in their despair, turn a
sort of master for themselves. Here, however, as
these parties have no shop to expose their goods
in, they must sell to those who have; and thus
finding *shop* purchasers, the trade now takes a new
complexion. The issue may be readily told. The
journeyman now becomes the competitor in a closer
sense than ever, with his fellow-journeyman; and
as the *cheapening* system widens, the work still
gets worse and worse done, and money *bulk*, not
money *worth*, becomes the only standard in the
business. London is at present the chief seat for
the manufacture of these sale women's shoes and
boots, though various establishments of the same
nature are growing up, day by day, throughout the
country. What the penny and twopenny paid
shirts are to the hapless needlewoman, the four-
penny and sixpenny-paid slippers are to the poor
sadly-miscalled *ladies*' shoemaker. The evil, too,
as connected with the London journeyman, and
those in other places, is still taking a worse phase
day after day. Leather, it is well known, as with
all other commodities, can be more profitably purchased in large than in small quantities; and hence

the master returns, in part, to his old character.
He now again gets ready his own materials, and
gives these to be manufactured by whom he pleases,
as was formerly the case; the only difference being,
that his cuttings-out are now in manifold pairs, for
a chance sale, and not, as before, to a separate
measure.   There is now, too, no other option for
the workman; he must do this work, and at the
very lowest wages, or *starve.*   He may, it is true,
considerably slight the articles; indeed, he *must* do
so, to live at all : and this is now his last and only
dependence.   And thus an art is found to retro-
grade, and the fair face of our social progress to
become spotted with these deeply-to-be-lamented
blemishes, the source of as much national demerit
and weakness, as they are of far-spread individual
misery.

The Northampton, Daventry, and Wellingbor-
ough wholesale manufacture of the man's shoe and
boot, may be traced to the same cause, and is as
productive of the like bad result.   The system has
grown in these places to a portentous bulk, and that
too in the short space of about a quarter of a century.   We see at present the goods of these places
in the shop-windows of almost every town in the
kingdom, ticketed up at so much the pair; the
prices charged being in many cases much less than

what some masters pay to the better-qualified journeyman for the mere making of similar-looking articles. The wealthier and more tasteful class of consumers still continue, however, to prefer bespeaking (or to have their measure taken for) their shoes and boots, than to run the risk of any of these chance bargains; and thus, so far, the trade maintains a certain degree of respectability, which is alike beneficial to both the employer and the employed.

The English boot and shoe about thirty years since, was generally speaking, the first article of its kind in the world, and so there was nothing to apprehend while the master's price was good and the workman's wages were good also; an evident decline, however, took place in the character of our workmanship. The Spectator of the 15th Dec., 1838, thus notices the absence of style in our boots and shoes : "A clumsy boot was till lately a distinguishing mark of a true Englishman abroad; now travellers get their feet neatly fitted in France, while all at home, who regard personal appearance, prefer French boots, and the predilection of the fair sex for shoes of Paris manufacture is notorious."

This competition has had the effect of improving the homemade article : but still it is easier to bawl for prohibiting duties than to beat the foreign work-

men out of the market. An intelligent cordwainer,
named James Devlin, an experienced workman of
a literary turn, has put forth a little book on the
boot and shoe trade of France, recommending to
his brethren of the craft the adoption of the French
method, which he describes with technical minuteness, and denouncing in his strictures on the character of English upper-leathers, the hurried and
careless process of the tanner and currier. What
Mr. Devlin says on the subject of leather, accounts
for the difference between a French boot that draws
on like a glove, and an ordinary English one that
confines the foot as in a vice, and hangs about the
leg like a clog. If we look to the nature of our
leather, excepting that used for the soles, we shall
find the article not so good as that which the
French bootmaker can purchase, and what, still
more pertinent to the matter is, that formerly it
was not so; confident I am, however, that a change
might be obtained, as well from the nature of our
raw hides and skins themselves, as from the ability
of the working currier; and, in proof of this, let
me instance the superior quality of our own jockey,
or topboot legs — so clear, so soft, and workable —
so handsomely grained, and so exquisitely drated.
No country can equal the British currier in this
particular, nor in the white leather, for the tops of

these boots; why his inferiority in other articles?
The reason is obvious: England, if not now, was
at least some years ago, the only jockey-boot nation *par excellence;* and hence, so far our superiority: the competition among us being so extensive
as to urge to the highest progressive perfection;
and that perfection always meeting its proper reward in the greater commands for orders.

Another fact to be attended to, is that in the boot
department, we have an inferior manner of blocking, or the turning the front-piece of our Wellington boot; in this we are far behind our neighbors.

Take up one of our bootfronts so prepared, and
compare it with a front coming from France (the
Bordeaux is the best), and the difference is as per-
ceptible as lamentable. How stiff, how dead, and
how forced, is the one; and how easy, moist, and
elastic, the other. The first, to one unskilled in
the operation, seems to be baked, rather than gently
moulded, when wet, into the position it has received; and then catch it by top and toe and pull it
ever so tenderly back, and lo! at once its crabbed
beauty is gone! and though you may press, push,
or contract it again into something of its original
form, still it can never be made to look the same as
before. Now, do the like to the French front;
nay, more, you need not pull it tenderly, but with

full force apply your strength to the two extremities, force it until it be straight, and then letting it go again, lay it on your board, and by a little application of the hand, it will nearly look as well as ever—no puckerings, no looseness, and still possessing the requisite curve.

Nothing can be more to the point than these strictures on the English leather and English blocking, as compared with the French. For the last seven years, I have in every order where calf-skin fronts have been required, used Bordeaux leather; it was not only soft, elastic, and durable, but in addition to the pleasure derived from making up a good article, it was as cheap as the English in the end, as we never had to put in a new front or repair cracks and breakages, a constant source of trouble and expense, incidental to the English fronts. It was no uncommon case, a few years since, after having bought the best article the trade could produce in calf-leather, after paying an extravagantly high price, and making up the article in the best possible manner, to find, after six or eight times wearing, a decided crack across the bend of the foot. I have tried every expedient on those occasions I could think of to prevent it, and acted on numerous suggestions from my foreman and workmen, and all to no purpose: not unfre-

quently the "most unkindest cut of all," has been
from the currier, who has laid the blame by turn
on the blocker, clicker, bootman; even the *feather**
has had to bear its share of the blame.

This inferiority of calfskin has not only been the
fault and disgrace of the British tanner and currier,
but his loss to an enormous amount; he has been
slow to admit it, but it is "a great fact;" a bright-
er day, however, now opens upon him.

Dr. Turnbull, after patient and repeated experiments on the science of tanning, has discovered
the true cause of all this hardness and breaking.
To him the tanners and the public owe a debt of
gratitude, which they will both best discharge by
patronising his invention.   I have had an opportunity of personally inspecting his process at Ber-
mondsey, from beginning to end, and I am enabled,
through his kindness, to convey the following information respecting his improved process of tanning :—

"The skins of the animals are composed of two
chief parts: the corium or cutis, and the cuticle or
epidermis.   The former, which is the true skin, is
a tissue of delicate fibres, crossing each other in all
directions, more thickly interwoven toward the surface, than in the deeper parts of the skin.   It is

* The *feather* is the edge of the insole.

8*

pervaded by a great number of conical channels,
the small extremities of which terminate at the ex-
ternal surface of the skin. These channels, which
are placed obliquely, contain nerves, secretory vessels, and cellular membranes.

"The cuticle or exterior covering is an insensible horny membrane, composed of several layers
of cells, devoid of blood-vessels.

"The process of tanning consists in the combination of the gelatinous substance of which the
skin is principally composed, and the tonic acid, or
tannin. The gelatinous substance in skins, and the
tannic acid, having a strong chymical affinity for
each other, the hide or skin is converted into
leather whenever tannin is brought into contact
with the gelatinous tissue or fibre.

"The slowness of the process in tanning leather,
and the imperfect manner in which it has hitherto
been accomplished, arise from the difficulty in
bringing the tannin or tannic acid into contact with
the gelatinous tissue, or fibre of the skins; and although, of late years, considerable modifications of
the old method of tanning have been introduced,
chiefly consisting in the employment of new materials, and the application of hydrostatic pressure,
yet the result, upon the whole, has been merely to
effect a saving of the time consumed in tanning,

and a consequent reduction of the price, without
any improvement in the quality of the leather, but
rather the reverse. This has given rise to a strong
prejudice in the minds of persons connected with
the leather trade, against leather tanned by any
quick process. The difficulty of bringing the tannin, or tannic acid, immediately and effectually into contact with the gelatinous fibre of the skin,
arises from several causes, which it may be useful
to enumerate.

"In preparing the skins and hides for the tanpit,
they are steeped for a considerable time in a solu-
tion of lime, to remove the hair and epidermis. In
this process, the skin imbibes a considerable quantity of lime, which has the effect of either removing
from the hide or skin, a portion of the gelatinous
substance, in the form of soluble gelatine, or, of al-
tering the gelatinous fibre, so as to render it inca-
pable of speedily and effectually combining with
the tannin or tannic acid, and the pores of the skin
are so impregnated with lime, as to prevent the
tanning principle from operating freely, or reaching the heart of the skins.

"The great object to be obtained, therefore, is
to find out some means of removing these obstructions and antagonistic principles, and of bringing
about a speedy and effectual combination of the

fibre of the hides or skins, and the tanning matter, and thus produce in a short space of time, leather superior in weight, quality, and durability, to any yet produced. The object of my improvements, is to remove these difficulties, and obstructions, either by extracting the lime with which hides and skins are impregnated in the process of removing the hair, or removing the same without the use of lime, by means not hitherto attempted."

The old plan of using lime, by which, no doubt, the skin was injured to an extent we never before supposed, and the consequent process in the tan-yard, of puring, as it is termed, by means of the dung of animals—a process the most filthy and disgusting, one would have thought, that could be imagined—gives way to Dr. Turnbull's discovery of "*sugar* and *sawdust*." This simple and delicate preparation, we are told, is more effectual; and "you may drink it," say the workmen, "for it is fit for any table in the land."

The new method is to prepare a mixture of sugar and water, and sawdust—it may be of any other substance containing saccharine matter, such as beetroot, potatoes, turneps, honey, &c. The action of the sugar and pyroxalic, or wood spirit, is so rapid, that the skins are rendered fit to receive and imbibe the tannic acid; and thus the operation of tanning is perfectly accomplished in a very short time. The leather thus produced is considerably heavier, and of finer quality, than any leather produced by the present method of tanning. This method of removing the lime is of immense importance, as it not only improves the leather in weight and durability, but enables the tanner to produce a superior article in a much less space of time, and at a much less expense, than heretofore. Attempts have been made to remove the lime by a preparation called grainer, which is mainly composed of the dung of animals. This being of a strong alkaline nature, necessarily destroys a considerable portion of the gelatinous matter, in the operation of extracting the lime; at the same time much injury is done to the texture of the skin by its rapid action in causing decomposition, and destroying the grain side of the skin, especially in summer. It must be obvious, however, that the moment the skin imbibes lime in any quantity, its effect and influence on the hide or skin are to a considerable extent permanent and destructive.

The advantages of the new method appear to be, first, a great additional weight of leather, especially in calfskins; second, leather of much better quality, soft and not liable to crack or strain; third, a considerable diminution in the expense; and fourth, the tanning is effected in one quarter of the time consumed by the present mode of tanning.

These improvements will, it is needless to say, prove of immense importance to our home manufacture, and now that the true principles of tanning skins comes to be understood, many other improvements will gradually suggest themselves. The Rouel leather, which is the name given to it by the doctor, is certainly the best article ever produced in England (I speak now of calfskin), and works up as fine or even finer than the French, without its accompaniment of dubbing, or its impost of 30 per cent.

In Queen Elizabeth's time, parliament busied itself much in matters of "leather and prunella;" numerous enactments being made, especially in reference to the former. A letter to lord-treasurer Burleigh, by W. Fleetwood, recorder of London, explains the opposition of the tanners to some enactments against them: "the one for lymyng [an old grievance, after all, this lyming], the other raisyng." He says: "All the excellencie and conning of a tanner consisteth in skilfull making of his owes [lyes;] surelie they must be many and severall and one stronger than another. The time of changing of the lether from one owes must be timed at proscribed hours, or else the lether will be utterly spoiled. My Lo, there be an infinite number of rules to be observed in tanning, the few which tanners did ever conceive, much less the parliament, who conveyed their information of such whiome nowe I do by experiens knowe not to be skilfull." A conclusion which many of good Queen Victoria's as well as Queen Bess's subject have arrived at, after parliamentary evidence and enactment, in matters which history, experience, and philosophy, have long since taught us, flourish *best* by being *let alone*.

CHAPTER V.

THE STRUCTURE OF THE HUMAN FEET, ETC.

"THERE is nothing more beautiful than the structure of the human foot," says Sir Charles Bell; "nor perhaps any demonstration which would lead a well-educated person to desire to know more of anatomy than that of the foot. The foot has in its structure all the fine appliances you see in a building. In the first place, there is an arch, in whatever way you regard the foot; looking down upon it, we perceive several bones coming round the astralagos, and forming an entire circle of surfaces in the contact. If we look at the profile of the foot, an arch is still manifest, of which the posterior part is formed by the heel, and the anterior by the ball of the great toe; and in the front, we find in that direction a transverse arch: so that, instead of standing, as might be imagined, on a solid bone, we stand upon an arch composed of a series of bones, which are united by the most curious provision for the elasticity of the foot; hence, if we jump from height directly upon the heel, a severe shock is felt; not so, if we alight upon the ball of the great toe, for there an elasticity is formed in the whole foot, and the weight of the body is thrown upon this arch, and the shock avoided."

Another writer, on the "diseases of the feet," thus alludes to the beauty and perfection of the human foot in its natural state :—

"The matchless forms of sculptured beauty which the destroying hand of time has left us in the works of the mighty masters of the classic time, exhibit to us the finest specimens of what the foot would be, if allowed its free and uninterrupted action.

"We are immediately struck with the admirable manner in which it is organized, both for the support of the frame and for motion; its flexibility, its power of action, its form, seem all to have been the result of the examination of the most perfect human models. We see that there have been no artificial coverings, no compression, no restraints; that the gait must have been free, firm, and elastic; that the natural and healthful action of every muscle, tendon, joint, and bone, was fully studied and expressed. There is no stiffness, no contraction of the heel or the sole of the foot; to the toes are given their proper functions; we see that only the sandal has been worn, merely to cover and protect

9

the integument under the broad and expanded foot,
there have been no ligatures, no unyielding band-
ages, no cramping compresses—all is alike free,
healthful, natural.

" We well can comprehend, on examining them,
how the Macedonian phalanx or the Roman legion,
performed its long day's march. We can see how
ten thousand Greeks pursued their daily wearying
course through the destroying climate of Asia,
marching firmly, manfully, alike across the arid
sand, the mountain pass, or the flinty plain.

" We are almost led to the wish to see the European soldier similarly prepared for his toilsome
march, unencumbered by the unyielding shoe,
which sometimes becomes in the day a source of
greater annoyance than of comfort to him. He
would be enabled to undertake fatigue and priva-
tions for which he is now totally unprepared. He
would find an elastic tread, a firm command over
his muscular system, follow upon such a plan. He
would be capable of making a charge upon the
enemy with greater steadiness, and enabled to bear
the shock which he is now less capable of resisting.
In this respect we should do well to imitate the
native soldier of India, who, under the English
banner, has followed a Clive, a Hastings, or a
Keane, when the British soldier has almost sunk

from the insuperable difficulties which attend wearing all parts of the dress he has been accustomed
to do in England, forgetful of the climate in which
he is placed."

For upward of twenty years as a bootmaker, I
have made the feet my study, and during that period
many thousand pairs of feet have received my attention. I have observed with minute care the *cast*
from the antique as well as " the modern instances,"
and I am obliged to admit, that much of the pain I
have witnessed, much of the distortion of the toes,
the corns on the top of the feet, the bunion on the
side, the callosities beneath, and the growing-in of
the nails between, are attributable to the shoemaker. The feet, with proper treatment, might be as
free from disease and pain as the hands ; their structure and adaptation to the wants and comfort of
man, as we have seen, is most perfect. Thirty-six
bones and thirty-six joints have been given by the
Creator to form one of these members, and yet man
cramps, cabins, and confines, his beautiful arrange-
ments of one hundred and forty-four bones and
joints, together with muscles, elastic cartilage,
lubricating oily fluid, veins, and arteries, into a pair
of shoes or boots, which, instead of protecting from
injury, produces the most painful as well as permanent results. Many volumes have been written on

the cause of corns, and it has been my lot to wade through many of them, without gaining much for my pains. I have therefore arrived at the conclusion, notwithstanding all that has been said to the contrary, that corns are in all cases the result of pressure.

I am confirmed in this opinion by one of the most respectable chiropodists of the present day (Mr. Durlacher), a gentleman who has had a considerable experience in the treatment of corns and bunions. He says :—

"Pressure and friction are unquestionably the predisposing causes of corns, although, in some instances, they are erroneously supposed to be hereditary. Improperly-made shoes invariably produce pressure upon the integuments of the toes and prominent parts of the feet, to which is opposed a corresponding resistance from the bone immediately beneath, in consequence of which the vessels of the dermis are compressed between them, become injured, congested, and, after a time, hypertrophied.

"When corns are produced by friction and slight pressure, they are the result of the shoes being too large and the leather hard, so that, by the extension of the foot, the little toe, or any prominent part, is constantly being rubbed and compressed by its own action.

"This may continue on and off for months, or even years, before any inconvenience is experienced, but, progressively, the cuticle increases, and is either detached from the dermis by serum being poured out between them, similar to a common blister, and a new covering produced, or the epidermis thickens into layers adhering to each other."

Chiropodists have been in the habit of classifying corns into—

1. Hard corns.
2. Soft corns.
3. Bleeding corns.

And these classes have been subdivided into many varieties, but it is enough, in a treatise on the feet and their covering, to allude to the cause of torment generally, as a hard substance and a soft one, pressing into the foot, as the Roman name emphatically describes it, "clavus dura"—a small tack.

The approach of a corn, as all who ever felt it know, commences with a slight inflammatory smart on the prominent part of the little toe; then comes on the excessive burning, the throbbing, the stabbing: "a little longer, yet a little longer;" and then the point of the tack begins to enter, the outer skin is penetrated, the next membrane becomes inflamed, and, from the delicate "network" of the

9*

rete mucosum, an increased quantity of secretion is
poured out: gradually a substance is formed, hard,
horny, and with a sharp point, that descends deeper and deeper into the foot, until not unfrequently
it reaches and enters the blood-vessels and very
joints themselves.

All attempts at cure must be directed to the
point of the corn. It has been usual to salve and
plaster and cut the head of this tack, generally
with little or no success—call it a thorn in the
foot, "spina pedum," a name given to it by some
practitioners; and how absurd this palliative treatment appears—every one knows that the thorn
must immediately be extracted, and if we delay,
great pain is the consequence, and soon nature ex-
pels it herself.

Some balsams and tinctures have been much
spoken of by the older writers on the different ex-
crescences, but modern practice has very judiciously excluded them, from their insufficiency to produce any good effect. The radical cure is more
dependent upon surgical than medical means.

"Although I have devoted," says Mr. Durlacher,
"nearly thirty years practical experience to the investigation, and have tried various chymical and
other remedial agents, yet I have never been able
to discover any certain cure for corns. Neverthe-

less, men are found bold enough in their ignorance and presumption, to assert, by public advertisement, that they possess an infallible nostrum, capable of thoroughly eradicating corns; and others who pretend to extract them, seek to aid their trickery and charlatanry by exhibiting small spiculæ as the roots of the corns they have extracted, although it is a positive fact from the structure of the skin, that such an assertion must be false, and the whole proceeding the veriest imposition imaginable."

The reader must, by this time have arrived at the conclusion, that the whole mischief is to be laid upon the covering of the feet, and not on the feet themselves. In some instances it may be admitted that the feet are peculiarly exposed to injury from the delicacy of the skin; some persons are constitutionally predisposed to corns, the slightest friction or pressure being sufficient to cause irritation, or, as in some cases, to develop a corn that has sometime been lying dormant. The illustrations given in former chapters of fashions, will sufficiently prove the cause of distortion of the feet; and the result of this infliction of pain for the sake of fashion, has been a plentiful harvest of corns.

Every one who has corns knows and feels that

pressure is the cause; "no one knows better where the shoe pinches, than he who wears it." Yet few persons know why it hurts, or are aware how the remedy should be applied.

Sometimes a shoe is too large, often too small, very often too short, but generally the wrong shape altogether. The fault is not so much in the shoes themselves, as in the lasts from which they are made; there the cause is to be found, and there it has been my study for many years to apply the remedy.

The best materials may have been used for sole and upper leather; the most exquisite closing and stabbing been put in till the work "looked like print;" the workmanship may have been "firstrate," but deficient in the primary and most essential part—the suitable form of the last on which the article was to be moulded. The boot or shoe would not be a suitable or comfortable covering for the foot, and the unfortunate wearer again finds that he has put his feet into the "shoe-maker's stocks."

Every one who wishes to be comfortably fitted, should have a pair of lasts made expressly for his own use; experience has taught me, and doubt-less many other masters who have had much to do with bespoke work for tender or peculiar feet,

that no plan is equal to this to secure a good fit
and save inconvenience and disappointment for
the future.

The length and the width are now every-day
affairs, but the judgment of fitting is another thing,
and here is the true skill.

A last fitted up to the length and width may do
or it may not; it may do by chance, or fail of
necessity; but if fitting be anything, it is a skilful adaptation of the last to the true form and re-
quirements of the foot generally.

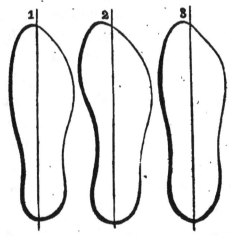

The outlines, 1, 2, 3, will show the direction
and bearing of three different feet, neither of
which would be comfortably fitted, if the length
and width were the only points attended to. For
No. 1, we require a straight-formed last, with an

equal proportion of wood on each side the centre line. No 2 requires considerable fulness of the inside joint, to allow for a bunion; the great toe requires a bed for the ball to rest in; the waist must be very hollow, else the quarter will bag; while No. 3 requires a wide flat tread and great thickness of wood, for the toes which are covered with corns.

Many persons have an idea that right and left shoes are a comparatively modern invention, but the illusions and illustrations to the contrary, in pages 39–44 disprove this; straight lasts are decidedly a modern invention, and notwithstanding what many persons say to the contrary, are decidedly inferior to a well-formed right and left pair.

The great evil has been that all right and left lasts, of late have been *crooked*. It was thought in abandoning the straight last with its faults, that a perfect fit could be secured in rights and lefts; and from one extreme, as is generally the case in fashion, the opposite was adopted, and a twisted right and left made the matter still worse.

It was thought nothing could be right and left but that which took a decided turn, and the consequence has been that for years lasts have been made with an ugly twist inward, where no wood was required, and on the outside, where the toes with all their tenderness and liability to injury have required thickness and breadth, nothing has been left.

I have pointed out this fault to last-makers a thousand times — have stood by them at their work, and have seen the part — where, of all things, I wished the room to be left — cruelly sliced off, or rasped away: the consequence to the unfortunate wearer of a shoe or boot made on that last must have been, months of torture.

Some workmen, however, have at last seen the error they have all along been committing, and adopted the improved form, wondering how it was never thought of before.

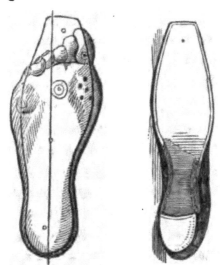

No. 1 represents a sketch of the foot and the sole

usually formed to fit it.   No. 2 is a well-formed sole, straight, suitable, and far more elegant.

The *straight* last has often been a better right and left for certain feet, than the *pair* made for them, the room having been given at the part most wanted, which was the chief thing : and although the hollow of the foot was not at all fitted, and the quarter gaped outside, yet it was easy.   On the other hand the right and left was deficient on the outside, and having nothing for the second, third, and little toe, they were cramped together, and the consequences were immediate pain, a hard corn on the joints of the little toe and a soft one between the others.

All this may be avoided.   The form of the feet should be taken in outline on a sheet of paper, and the prominent toes noted down at the time, and immediately after a pair of lasts made suitable in every way.

But instead of this, hundreds of shoemakers in the country have been making all their lifetime, from some old misshapen pieces of wood, that perhaps had done service to their fathers and grandfathers, and been patched and altered to suit the wants of a whole parish.   Even in town, where we have last-makers at our elbow, we have been far from doing what we ought in this matter.   Instead

of fitting the foot to the shoe, the business of the
tradesman certainly is to shape his last so correctly
that the shoe should fit the foot.

Petrarch is said to have nearly lamed himself
from the attempts he made, and the pinching he
underwent, to display to his Laura a neat foot.
Cases of this kind are frequently met with every
day, where every sacrifice is made for this end, and
pinching all over the foot may be tolerated, and no
bad consequences ensue for a time; but the pinching at one place is the point which ought immediately to be "reformed altogether."

It is extremely amusing to witness, on the other
side, the care some old gentlemen take to get their
shoes made easy; while the Petrarch of the present day, orders his boots to be *smart*, and threatens
his bootmaker that if he can get into them, he
"won't have 'em," the old gentleman of experience
and wisdom comes with two pairs of thick lamb's
wool stockings on, which his friend who accompa-
nies him waggishly says, are—

> " His youthful hose well saved, a world too wide
>   For his shrunk shank ;"

he looks knowingly in return and whispers, that he
put on two pairs of the thickest stockings he had,
on purpose to deceive the shoemaker.

In the early English translation of " Lazarillo de Tormes," is this passage : " If you bid a shoemaker who has been thirty years at his trade make a new pair of shoes with broad toes, high in the instep, and tight about the heel, he must pare your feet before he pleases you"—a sly, but sarcastic allusion to the imperfect fitting of the shoemaker, and an admission of the pride of the wearer.

Ladies and gentlemen, and even children, should have their own lasts, and be sure they are carefully and correctly made to the feet.

It would, however, be expecting too much that for a single pair of shoes or boots, a shoemaker or bootmaker should make for his customer a pair of lasts, free of charge; as prices are now, he would be a considerable loser—the customer might never favor him with another order, he seeks a cheaper shop—goes abroad or dies. The lasts on which a skilful workman has been employed for perhaps a whole day, and which cost at least four or five shillings, are left on his hands perfectly useless.

For my own personal comfort I would weigh my own lasts which have been carefully made, in a scale against their weight in silver, and consider them cheap; numbers of our nobility and gentry, in effect, do the same, and to a much greater amount, for their personal comfort, in matters of the teeth, eyes, chest, hair, hands, and ears. Then why not a little sacrifice, a little more liberality, to those important members—the feet.

No such remuneration, however, as I have hinted at would be expected; five or six shillings generally would remunerate the maker of a pair of lasts, and the better the fit the greater satisfaction to all.

We have now seen the fashions from the earliest period; many of the shoes from their form and material must have been comfortable; the broad shoe of Henry VIII., wood engraving p. 46, was one of that class, and the slashed specimens in p. 47 sufficiently show where the shoe pinched in 1577, and how relief was sought and obtained : even the very worst of all the fashions might have been made comparatively comfortable had due attention been paid to the form of the lasts.

The poet Gay gives a caution on this matter, and if the value I attach to my lasts be their weight in silver, I am free to confess Gay's lines are worth their weight in *gold.*

> " Let firm well-hammered soles protect thy feet,
> Through freezing snows and rains and soaking sleet.
> Should the big last extend the shoe too wide,
> Each stone will wrench the unwary step aside ;
> The sudden turn may stretch the swelling vein,
> The cracking joint unhinge, or ankle sprain ;
> And, when too short the modest shoes are worn,
> You 'll judge the seasons by your shooting corn."

CHAPTER VI.

THAT any form of boot or shoe should have interfered with the beauty of the human foot and its elastic tread, is much to be lamented. The sculptures of antiquity all show great symmetry and beauty of form, whether in the male or female foot: the plump, rounded, and truly natural shape of the feet of the Venus de Medicis has excited the admiration of every one who ever looked at that beautiful statue.

Poets in all ages have been lavish in their praises of the "human foot divine," and a volume of extracts might be made on the poetry of the feet. The inspired Isaiah breaks forth—"How beautiful on the mountains are the feet of him that bringeth glad tidings." Kitto says, in his remarks on this passage, "When the person is very eminent for rank or holiness, the mention of the feet rather than any other part of the person denotes the respect or reverence of the speaker; and then, also, an epithet of praise or distinction is given to the feet, of which, as the most popular instance, the 'golden feet' of the Burmese monarch forming the title by which he is usually named by his subjects."

Homer pays homage in the Iliad to Thetis, whom he calls "the silver-footed queen."

Bathus, in the Tenth Idyllium of Theocritus, exclaims :—

> "Charming Bombyce, you my numbers greet,
> How lovely, fair, and beautiful your feet !"

While Paris in making choice of the many beautiful virgins brought before him, pays particular attention to their pedal attractions :—

> "Their gait he marked as gracefully they moved,
> And round their feet his eye sagacious roved."

Ben Jonson describes a lover whose affection for his mistress was so great that he—

> ———"would adore the shoe,
> And slipper was left off, and kiss it too."

and again—

> "And where she went the flowers took thickest root,
> As she had sowed them with her odorous foot."

Butler, too, has the same springing up of flowers in his "Hudibras":—

> "Where'er you tread, your foot shall set
> The primrose and the violet."

In an anonymous volume of poems printed in

10*

1653, the writer being contemporary with Butler, we find the following beautiful sentiment:—

> "How her feet tempt; how soft and light she treads,
> Fearing to wake the flowers from their beds:
> Yet from their sweet green pillows everywhere
> They start and gaze about to see my fair.
>
> *   *   *   *   *
>
> Look how that pretty modest columbine
> Hangs down its head to view those feet of thine!
> See the fond motion of the strawberrie
> Creeping on earth we go along with thee;
> The lovely violet makes after too,
> Unwilling yet, my dear, to part with you.
> The knot-grass and the daisies catch thy toes
> To kisse my faire one's feet before she goes."

Shakspere, in " Troilus and Cressida," describes Diomede walking:—

> "'T is he, I ken the manner of his gait;
> He rises on the toe; that spirit of his,
> In aspiration lifts him from the earth!"

Again:—

> "Shore's wife hath a pretty foot;"

and his graphic description of a free-natured woman—

> ——"nay, her foot speaks."

Old Herrick, who seems to have had the finest perception of the delicate and charming, thus compliments Mrs. Susanna Southwood:—

> "Her pretty feet,
> Like smiles, did creep
> A little out, and then,
> As if they started at bo-peep,
> Did soon draw in again."

It is the exquisite intimation of the lively character of the inward spirit, shown in the active movements of the feet, which Sir John Suckling has imitated in his ballad of the Wedding:—

> "Her feet beneath her petticoat
> Like little mice stole in and out,
> As if they feared the light;
> But oh, she dances such a way,
> No sun upon an Easter day
> Is half so fine a sight!"

Very beautiful also is the following, from one of our old poets. The words are given entire, in Wilson's "Cheerful Ayres for three Voices." Who could do any harm to so beautiful a part of the human frame?

> "Doe not feare to put thy feet
> Naked in the river sweet;
> Think not newt, nor leech, nor toade,
> Will bite thy foot where thou hast trode."

These pretty allusions to pretty feet might be multiplied to a great extent; they will, however, suffice to show the homage paid by all true poets to these useful and beautiful members.

I come now to the more practical part of the

subject, and will, to the best of my ability, say a
few, words to the ladies respecting boots and shoes
of the present day. I am of opinion that the best
coverings for the feet are boots; not only do they
look neat and tidy, but the general and gradual
support they give all over the feet and ankles in-
duces strength and gives tone to the veins and
muscles. Shoes, on the contrary, and especially
long-quartered ones, require a great effort from the
muscles to be kept on, and this, when long applied,
tires and weakens. The lace and button boots usually worn need not be described; they are very good
and suitable to most feet, and, if cut well and lasted
properly, generally give comfort and satisfaction.
The trouble, however, of lacing and unlacing, the
tag coming off, the button breaking, or the shank
hurting, the holes soon wearing out, and many other little annoyances, have all been experienced as
bores by thousands who have worn that kind of boot.

About ten years since I first thought of an elastic boot, that might possibly remedy in a great
measure all these minor evils, and combine many
advantages never possessed by any former boot. I
am not, however, sure that an elastic boot was not
known at a very early period in England.

The following passage from Chaucer seems to
favor the idea :—

"Of shoon and boot'es new and faire,
   Look at least thou have a paire,
   And that they fit so fetously,*
   That these rude men may utterly
   Marvel, sith they sit so plain,
   How they come on and off again."

What this boot could have been, we are now at
a loss to know, and unfortunately the paintings and
sculptures of antiquity, are not sufficiently clear in
these little matters of texture and material, to gain
any information: no such boot has, however, been
known in our time, or many centuries before.

My first experiments were a failure, as the manufacture of elastic materials was not so perfect as
they are at the present period, and the necessary
elasticity could not be gained in any material I
could meet with. The difficulty was to get an In-
dia-rubber web so elastic that the boot would go
on and off, and yet not so soft and yielding as that
it would not return again to its original form—my
object being not only—,

"That these rude men may utterly
   Marvel, sith they sit so plain,
   How they come on and off again,"

but that they should "sit plain" and "fit fetously"
as well after they were on.

After several experiments in wire and India-rub-

* Properly.

ber, I succeeded in getting the exact elasticity required, and subsequent improvements in materials and workmanship, have combined to make the elastic boot the most perfect thing of its kind.

I am indebted to the countess of Blessington, and Lady Charlotte Bacon, for some of the earliest hints and suggestions for its improvement; also to Mrs. S. C. Hall, the Baroness de Calabrella, and other ladies of literary fame, who were among the first to patronise the invention. One of my earliest customers, a lady of great originality of thought and expression, first induced me to make it an article of universal sale, by saying:—

"These boots are the comfort of my life, if you were only to give them a sounding name—if you like, call them *lazy boots* and turn it into *Greek*—all the world will buy them, and you'll make your fortune."

For many years I have scarcely made any other kind of boots but the elastic; but, I have not made a fortune. I am happy, however, if in any way I have contributed to the comfort of my fellow-creatures, or been instrumental in affording employment to my own countrymen.

Her majesty has been pleased to honor the invention with the most marked and continued patronage; it has been my privilege for some years to make boots of this kind for her majesty, and no one who reads the court circular, or is acquainted with her majesty's habits of walking and exercise in the open air, can doubt the superior claims of the elastic over every other kind of boots; it has been well remarked, "the road to health is a foot-path."

The materials for making ladies' boots have been various, the best of course have been those which combine strength with a thin delicate texture; for strong double or cork sole boots, cloth, kerseymere, or cashmere; for single sole, summer, or dress boots, silk, satin, and an improved prunella, with a twilled silk back, is best.

The neatest, firmest, and the coolest material I have ever used is a silk web, called *stocking-net;* this I have had woven in black and colors, and as it readily moulds to the form of the foot, and can be made up without seams, it is a favorite material with her majesty, and the most distinguished ladies of her court: this boot would appear to be the veritable "boote newe and faire" of old Chaucer's time, so thoroughly light, elastic, and graceful, as it is to a pretty foot.

The leather best adapted for ladies' boots is morocco or goat-skin, which, when properly dressed, is sufficiently strong and durable—kid being the skin of the young goat, is naturally finer and more delicate; the enamel or varnish leather, commonly called *patent*, is also very suitable, and being made of calf-skin, is strong. For the little toecaps and golashes of ladies' boots it answers admirably, and as it requires no cleaning, always looks well, and the upper part of the boot is kept clean and tidy.

Some ladies, however, can not bear any leather—the material best adapted for such is the Pannus-corium, or leather-cloth. This invention has met with very extensive patronage from a class whose feet require something softer even than the softest leather.

As it resembles the finest leather in appearance, and has many of the best properties of the usual cordovan, and not having like it to be tanned and curried, it does not draw the feet; its peculiar softness and pliability, therefore, at once commend it to the notice of those persons who have corns and tender feet.

One very important thing to be attended to, is, that the golashes and toecaps of all boots should come *above* or *below* the joint of the great toe. Very frequently the edge of the leather comes at the very worst part of the foot; and, strange enough, sometimes we see a hard seam put exactly on the corn, and running across the bunion. If no leather be put at all, the boot or shoe being made entirely of stuff, frequently a secret enemy lurks between the outside and the lining, in the shape of a leather side-lining; weeks pass on perhaps without your being aware of its presence; at last, from the heat and perspiration of the feet, this side-lining becomes as hard as horn, and great pain is the consequence.

Shortly after the elastic boot was brought out, I made a little improvement in shoes, which are now made wholly or partially elastic. They are well suited for ladies whose feet swell, or whose insteps rise very suddenly, as they accommodate themselves to those changes. Morocco, prunella, and leather shoes, may all be made comfortable by attending to the instructions contained in the previous chapter on the proper forms of lasts.

The elastic clog is another improvement on the old mode of fastening with straps, buckles, and buttons; clogs on this principle are put on and taken off without any trouble or fastening, and by

11

a very simple arrangement of a plush back, all chafing of the boot is avoided and great firmness secured, without a chance of their slopping.

Ladies should always have a pair of these clogs ready to slip on—as they wonderfully save the boots in dirty weather; and, after having worn the elastic boot for some days and found the great support it gives to the ankles, how easily it remedies undue swelling and enlargement of the veins, and prevents frequently that serious disease, varicose veins, no one would like, nor is it advisable, immediately on returning home after a dirty walk, to throw off the boots; the remedy is then found in the clogs or golashes; you put them on over your thin ordinary boots, and thus protected, you may go where you please, and taking them off on your return home, walk in on the finest carpet without a chance of soiling or injuring it.

CHILDREN'S BOOTS AND SHOES.

The attention of every mother should be given to the state of her child's feet. How much subsequent pain, distortion, and lameness, might be spared, if a little consideration were given in time to the child's shoes and boots. As a general rule, if proper length and width be given, all will be well;

but this must be seen to frequently, as little feet soon grow larger.

If shoes are worn, they should be easy across the toes, and of good form in the sole, hollow and arched at the waist, and snug at the heel—if boots, then the elastic the same as ladies'.

If the ankles are weak, a surgeon should be consulted without delay. I have benefited many children by making an elastic lace boot, which, from the support it affords, compressing the muscles of the foot, and by bearing well up by means of a spring under the arch of the foot, has prevented lameness, and restored the feet and ankles to their natural form.

GENTLEMEN'S BOOTS AND SHOES.

The foregoing remarks on ladies' boots, apply equally to gentlemen's half-boots, the same materials being used for dress or summer walking; they need, therefore, only to be referred to in their proper place, and the remarks and illustrations, pages 105–108, will convey all that is necessary to know of the proper shape and true principles of fitting, sufficient length, straightness of form, and the room in the right place, being the chief points to be attended to.

Shoes are now very little worn; boots of some

kind or other being the general wear. At present,
says the author of "The Shoemaker," we are emphatically a booted people; so are the French and
the Americans; the fashion goes onward with the
great progress of civilization; it is as it were its
very sign. Homer has applied to his own far-fam-
ous countrymen, the epithet of the *well-booted
Greeks*, a somewhat singular coincidence at first
sight, though doubtless he meant no more than
some sort of stiff leg-covering, as.a protection necessary to the warriors of whom he sang, and bearing no likeness to the gay delicate boot of later.
times.

The fame of the English in this way is not, however, altogether new; though from what the present generation must have observed since the introduction of the Wellington, it may seem to be otherwise. We were, it appears, a booted people
before, or at least were so considered.

"I will amaze my countrymen," said Gondemar,
Spanish ambassador, to the court of James I., "by
letting them know on my return that all London is
booted, and apparently ready to walk out of town."
The reflection certainly is curious; the old poets
and heroes were booted, and the hero of Waterloo
has given as proud a distinction to our own boot.
But then people in past days, when they had their

boots on, were thought to look prepared for a journey, whereas, at present, the boot is almost as domestic a thing as the slipper.   We go to the ball-room in it, the theatre, the houses of parliament, and even royalty itself is approached in the boots!

The Wellington is unquestionably the most gentlemanly thing of its kind, and all the attempts of the Bluchers, Alberts, Clarences, Cambridges, and such like, to rival it, most signally fail.   Its well-known character for style, wear, and facility of repair, has stamped it the boot of the present day.

A good Wellington boot of the softest calf-leather, the sole moderately thick, the waist hollow and well-arched, firm and yet flexible, cut to go on without dragging all your might with boothooks, and made with an intermediate sole of felt to prevent creaking, is the best boot for general wear that can be made.

The varnished or patent leather Wellington, is a handsome article of the same class, and is generally made with a tongue, the legs being of colored morocco leather.   It is now brought to a great state of perfection, and our bootclosers are the most perfect in the matter of fancy-closing and stabbing, in Europe.

For many years, this department of the trade has been quite distinct from shoemaking, or boot-

11*

making. Originally, closing, making the boot, shoe, and slipper, and even ladies' and children's shoes, was the work of one individual; now they are separate branches, and the closer has not only risen in this country, but his work is universally celebrated from this circumstance, for its strength and beauty. Perhaps nothing in the way of workmanship is equal to what is termed *blind-stabbing:* the leather, held between the workman's knees, is pierced with a small pointed awl, which he holds together with the flax or silken thread that is to follow, in his right hand; his left on the inside of the bootleg, and *in the dark*, in an instant sends through the bristle, and receives through the same little hole the point of the right hand one; the thread is drawn, the stitch formed, quickly another hole is made, and the same operation repeated.

Nothing in the way of sewing or stitching, can equal this blind-stabbing, one half of which is done in the dark, the skill being acquired by constant practice, and the extreme delicacy of the touch; from twenty to thirty stitches have been done to the inch in this way, and in *prize-work* as many as sixty, every stitch being clear, sharply defined, and beautifully regular.

THE ELASTIC BOOT FOR GENTLEMEN, is a light and easy article; it does not encumber the leg, and, unlike the half-and-half Clarence, with its valve of folded leather, and all kinds of holes and contrivances, it fits the ankle like a stocking, and readily yields and elasticates to every motion of the feet and legs.

The cut represents an elastic boot with a golosh of leather all round, the upper part being cloth, silk, prunella, cashmere, kid, or the silk-stocking net; the material generally determining the kind of boot it is to be, and the thickness of the sole. When it is required that the elastic boot should have the appearance of a Wellington, it is made entirely of leather, spring and all, and thus made, when on the foot, has every appearance of it, as no join is ever detected above the instep, when the trowsers accidentally rise a little higher than the wearer of a would-be Wellington sometimes wishes them.

Travellers find these boots great comforts, they take up very little room in the portmanteau, are

soon cleaned, and are on and off in an instant; if
made of patent leather, they need only a wipe with
an old silk handkerchief. No boothooks are ever
required, the best hooks being nature's own, the
fingers, and the only bootjack ever wanted, is
the toe of one boot applied to the heel of the
other.

Dress Pumps are almost the only shoes now
worn; they are generally made of patent leather,
and should be cut to sit well at the quarters.

The *Oxonian Shoe* is, however, a very useful article, and if properly made, is the best shoe for
walking and for wear. It laces up in front with
three or four holes, and sits snug about the quarters and heel; the vamp comes well above the joint,
and never hurts, by seams or pressure, the little
toes: if it were not for the seam across the instep,
girding and making it difficult to get the shoe on,
and the frequent breaking at that part from the
strain it undergoes, no shoe could be better.

I have, however, effected a great improvement in
it, which remedies the evil at once, gives great freedom in putting on, and entirely prevents the breaking of the seam and vamp; this improvement would,
however, be hardly intelligible from description,
and must therefore be seen to be understood properly. For shooting, and strong wear, it will be

found extremely suitable, and it is perhaps the best
of all shoes for young gentlemen.

STOCKINGS, WASHING THE FEET, &c.—Much
more of comfort to the feet depends on the stockings than people are aware of; nothing can be
worse than a stocking too large or too small, the
more common case is its largeness, and when I see
a cotton or thread stocking tucked under at the toe,
and by the perspiration of the foot and the tread,
become quite hard and compact, a hard ridge of a
seam pressing on the toes, which show the marks
produced by the pressure all over the surface, I
wonder how persons *can* expect comfort.

The best stockings for general wear, are those
made of lamb's wool, vigonia, and Shetland knit.
The pedestrian well knows the difference on a long
day's walk, between a cotton or linen stocking and
one of wool; he knows that the former soon becomes hard, damp, and chilly, with the moisture of
the foot, whereas the latter enables him to bear fatigue, defends his foot from the friction of the shoe,
secures it from blisters, and in every way ministers
to his comfort.

Persons, however, who do not use much exercise may indulge in a silk stocking; ladies will not
only find this the most elegant of all coverings for
the feet, but at the same time far more comfortable

than either cotton or linen. If the best silk is considered too expensive, then a thick spun silk is a good substitute.

The frequent change of the stockings conduces much to comfort, and they should, in cases of corns or tender feet, be worn inside-out; even the little seam of a stocking has aggravated in a great measure a corn just appearing, which but for that pressure, might soon have been got rid of.

Let the feet be bathed at least three times a week in tepid or cold water. For some years I was in the habit of making easy shoes for the late Sir Astley Cooper. That eminent surgeon never cramped his feet, nor wore shoes that would give him pain; but one thing, however, he habitually accustomed himself to, and that was to immerse his feet in cold water as soon as he arose, and use a rough towel freely afterward.

In the coldest day of winter, he was to be seen without a great coat, with silk stockings on his legs, and short breeches, traversing the court of the hospital, or sitting in his carriage.

The sponge should be applied to the feet, and between the toes, round the nails, which should be cut just to a level with the toe-end, and then a good rubbing all over with a dry towel, a little Eau de Cologne to finish off, and you feel quite another creature.

Every care should be taken that the insensible perspiration of the feet should be encouraged and allowed to pass off freely. Dr. Wilson, in his "Practical Treatise on Healthy Skin," says : "To arrive at something like an estimate of the value of the perspiratory system, in relation to the rest of the organism, I counted the perspiratory pores on the palm of the hand, and found 3,528 to the square inch, (on the heel where the ridges are coarser 2,268). Now each of these pores being the aperture of a little tube of about a quarter of an inch long, it follows that in a square inch of skin, there exists a length of tube equal to 882 inches, or 73½ feet. Surely, such an amount of drainage as 73 feet in every square inch of skin, assuming this to be the average for the whole body, is something wonderful, and the thought naturally intrudes itself what if this *drainage* were obstructed ?"

This is too often the case, improper shoes and waterproof materials, not only check the natural evaporation of the skin, but eventually produce diseases of the feet in the worst form ; nothing so much conduces to general comfort, as the feet and ankles being in a healthy state, and few things tell upon the manners and temper more than constant pain and irritability of the extremities.

The fashions of boots and shoes have met with

their share of our attention and research, the errors
of form and make have been pointed out, the best
remedies have been suggested, it now only remains
for us to adhere as closely to nature's laws as possible.   Art may do much, but even Miss Kilman-
segg's "precious leg" of pure gold, was but a poor
substitute for her more precious lost one.

> " Peace and ease, and slumber lost,
>   She turned, and rolled, and tumbled, and tossed,
>   With a tumult that would not settle ;
>   A common case indeed with such,
>   As have too little, or think too much,
>   Of the precious and glittering metal.

> " Gold ! she saw at her golden foot,
>   The peer whose tree had an olden root,
>   The proud, the great, the learned to boot,
>   The handsome, the gay, and the witty —
>   The man of science, of arms, of art,
>   The man who deals but at pleasure's mart,
>   And the man who deals in the city."

(1.) Many are the hints thrown out by some of
our old herbalists, in their quaint language, as to
the power of some of our indigenous herbs.   One
which has certainly some slight influence on corns,
and is a great favorite among the popular writers
on corns, is the common house-leek, the *sedum*

murale. This herb which is found growing on the tops of old garden-walls and upon the roofs of houses, has a leaf of considerable thickness, owing to the large quantity of cellular tissue between its upper and lower lamina, in whose interstices is found considerable juice, which abounds with hydrochloric acid in a free and uncombined state. Owing, doubtless, to the presence of the acid, the juice acts upon the indurated mass, softening and destroying the surface, but leaving the lower parts as great a source of mischief as ever, and sometimes converting the corn into a more hardened mass than it was before.—*The Diseases of the Feet.*

(2.) "There is another way of disposing of a corn," says Mr. Erasmus Wilson, "which I have been in the habit of recommending to my friends; it is effectual, and obviates the necessity for the use of the knife. Have some common sticking-plaster spread on buff leather; cut a piece sufficiently large to cover the corn and skin around, and have a hole punched in the middle of exactly the size of the summit of the corn. Now take some common soda of the oil-shops, and make it into a paste, with about half its bulk of soap; fill the hole in the plaster with this paste, and cover it with a piece of sticking-plaster. Let this be done at bed-time, and in the morning remove the plaster, and wash the

12

corn with warm water. If this operation be repeated every second, third, or fourth day, for a
short time, the corn will be removed. The only
precaution required to be used is to avoid causing
pain; and so long as any tenderness occasioned by
the remedy lasts, it must not be repeated. When
the corn is reduced within reasonable bounds by
either of the above modes, or when it is only threat-
ening, and has not yet risen to the height of being
a sore annoyance, the best of all remedies is a
piece of soft buff leather, spread with soap-plaster,
and pierced in the centre with a hole exactly the
size of the summit of the corn."

(3.) It is usually the custom to soak the corns
previously to cutting them. As this is not always
convenient, the following method of rendering the
corn soft will serve instead. Take a strip of wash-
leather, of size sufficient to cover the corn, and a
strip of oiled silk rather larger; wet the leather
and apply it to the corn, then cover it with the oiled
silk, which will prevent the leather from becoming
dry. Keep this on for a few days, wetting the
leather two or three times a day. This will render
the corn so soft that the razor may be applied without causing pain.

CHAPTER VII.

THE first settlers of New England, Virginia, and other British colonies in America, brought with them to this country, the fashions of dress which were prevalent in England at the time of their emigration, being the same as described in the preceding pages, with regard to boots and shoes in use in the seventeenth century, in the reigns of the Stuarts, or under the dominion of the commonwealth, when Cromwell was at the head of affairs. New England being settled by the puritans, the dresses of the first English inhabitants of that section were of a plainer character than those of Virginia and other colonies, where the first settlers were cavaliers, or adherents of the house of Stuart.

The dress, particularly the boots and shoes, worn by the earlier settlers of New England, are thus described by Miss Caulkins, in her "History of Norwich, Connecticut." "The shoes worn in 1689, were coarse, clumped, square-toed, and adorned

with enormous buckles. If any boots made their
appearance, prodigious was the thumping as they
passed up the aisles of the church; for a pair of
boots was then expected to last a man's life. The
tops were short, but very wide at the top; formed,
one might suppose, with a special adaptation to
rainy weather; collecting the water as it fell, and
holding an ample bath for the feet and ankles!

" It is uncertain whether the small clothes had
then begun to *grow*, so as to reach below the knee,
and to be fastened with knee-buckles or not. The
earlier mode was to have them terminate above the
knee, and to be tied with ribands. The common
kind were made of leather. Red woollen stockings
were much admired. Swords were customarily
worn when in full dress, by all the earlier settlers
of New England, both in a civil and a military
capacity. Hats were at that time made of wool;
perhaps two or three at the church door reverently
took off a black 'beaverett,' though that was a
costly article in those days. The coat was made
with a long straight body, falling below the knee,
and with no collar. The waistcoat was long."

As necessity is the mother of invention, many of
the earlier settlers of New England, where mechan-
ics were scarce, were accustomed to manufacture
their own clothing, including boots and shoes.

The more wealthy inhabitants imported their clothing from England, but the farmers generally made in their own families most of the articles required for clothes. Individuals who were expert in shoemaking, many of them self-taught, were sometimes employed by farmers and others to make up a stock of shoes for the family, once or twice a year. These persons journeyed about from house to house, in the winter season, taking their tools on their backs. Leather was occasionally imported from England, but as population in the colonies increased, tanneries were established, particularly in the large towns.

A writer in the Old Colony Memorial, gives the following account of dress among the early inhabitants of New England :—

"In general, men, old or young, had a decent coat, vest, and small clothes, and some kind of fur hat. Old men had a great-coat and a pair of boots. The boots generally lasted for life. For common use they had a long jacket, reaching about half way to the thigh; flannel shirts, woollen stockings, and thick leather shoes ; a silk handkerchief for holydays, which would last ten years. Shoes and stockings were not worn by the young men, and by but few men in the farming business.

" As for boys, as soon as they were taken out of petticoats, they were put into small clothes, summer or winter. This continued until long trowsers were introduced, which they called *tongs*. They were but little different from our pantaloons. These were made of tow-cloth, linen, cotton, or flannel-cloth, and soon were used by old men and young.

" The women, old and young, wore flannel gowns in the winter. The young women wore, in the summer, wrappers or shepherdress; and about their ordinary business, did not wear stockings and shoes. They were usually contented with one calico gown; but they generally had a calimanco gown, another of camlet, and some had them made of poplin. The sleeves were short, and did not come below the elbow. On holydays, they wore one, two, or three ruffles on each arm—the deepest of which were sometimes nine or ten inches. They wore long gloves, coming up to the elbow. Round gowns had not then come in fashion; so they wore aprons. The shoes were either of thick or thin leather, broadcloth, or worsted stuff, all with heels an inch and a half high, with peaked toes turned up in a point. They generally had small, very small muffs, and some wore masks."

The following extracts from Watson's Annals of New York, will further elucidate the fashions as to boots and shoes in the British colonies in America.

" Before the revolution, no hired man or woman

wore any shoes as fine as calf-skin; that kind was
the exclusive property of the gentry. The servants
wore coarse neat's leather. The calf-skin then had
a white rind of sheep-skin stitched into the top
edge of the sole, which they preserved white, as a
dress-shoe, as long as possible."

The use of boots has come in since the war of
independence; they were first worn with black
tops, after the military, strapped up in union with
the knee buttons; afterward bright tops were introduced. The leggings to these latter were made
of buckskin for some extreme beaux, for the sake
of close fitting a well-turned leg.

"Boots were rarely worn; never as an article of
dress; chiefly when seen, they were worn by host-
lers and sailors; the latter always wore great petti-
coat trowsers, coming only to the knee and then
tying close. Common people wore their clothes
for a much longer time than now; they patched
their clothes much and long; a garment was only
'half worn' when it became broken.

"As English colonists we early introduced the
modes of our British ancestors. They derived their
notions of dress from France.

"Breeches, close fitted, with silver, stone, or
paste gem buckles; shoes or pumps, with silver
buckles of various sizes and patterns; thread,

worsted, and silk stockings, were worn in the colonies previous to the revolution. The poorer class wore sheepskin and buckskin breeches close set to the limbs."

A glance at any of the numerous engravings copied from Colonel Trumbull's national painting, the "Declaration of Independence," shows the dress of gentlemen in this country during the American revolution; namely, small clothes fastened below the knee with buckles, the leg covered only with stockings, the shoes fastened with large buckles. This fashion continued until the close of the eighteenth century, when pantaloons and boots were introduced from France. Mr. Sullivan, in his "Familiar Letters," says : "About the end of the eighteenth century, the forms of society underwent considerable change. The levelling process of France began to be felt. Powder for the hair began to be unfashionable. A loose dress (pantaloons) for the lower limbs was adopted. Wearing the hair tied was given up, and short hair became common. Colored garments went out of use, and dark or black were substituted. Buckles disappeared. The style of life had acquired more of elegance, as means had increased."

A sketch of the manner in which Washington, Jefferson, Hamilton, and other public men, dressed, is given by Mr. Sullivan, in the work above quoted, and the following extracts may be interesting to our readers :—

"Washington, at his levees, while president [from 1789 to 1797], dressed in black velvet, his hair powdered and gathered behind in a silk bag, yellow gloves on his hands ; holding a cocked hat, with a cockade in it, and the edges adorned with a black feather. He wore knee and shoe buckles, and a long sword, with a polished steel hilt. The scabbard was white polished leather."

"Jefferson, in 1797, wore a black coat and light under clothes. He was then fifty-four years of age."

"Hamilton, in 1795, being then in his thirty-eighth year, wore at a dinner party, a blue coat, with bright buttons and long skirts, a white waistcoat, black silk small clothes, white silk stockings," (and shoes, of course).

The Hessian or Austrian boot, described in the preceding pages, which was first used in England, about the year 1789, was soon afterward introduced into the United States, as was the white-top boot, which came into fashion in England, early in the

reign of George III. This latter was generally
worn with small clothes, and more frequently by
elderly gentlemen than young men. The Hessian
or half-boot was made with a seam in the back, and
was worn over pantaloons fastened around the ankle with ribands or galloons. After a few years,
it gave way to the Suwarrow boot, so named after

Suwarroff, a Russian general, celebrated for his
campaigns in Turkey, Poland, Italy, &c. He died
in 1800; soon after which time the Suwarrow boot
was introduced into England and the United States.
This boot was worn by citizens, as well as in the
army and navy; it was made with a seam at each

side, and reached nearly to the knee. In front it was scolloped, and ornamented with a black silk tassel. Sometimes gold tassels were worn by military and naval officers in full dress. We recollect having seen Commodore Decatur, while his ship, the United States, lay in the river Thames, in Connecticut, during the war of 1812, wear a pair of elegant Suwarrow boots, with gold tassels, on an occasion of his being invited to a dinner party in Norwich.

The Suwarrow boot continued in fashion for about fifteen years, when, after the battle of Waterloo, it was superseded by the Wellington boot, which it is well known was named after the duke of Wellington. This boot seems to have settled the laws of fashion respecting the feet, as decisively as the battle of Waterloo settled the affairs of Europe.

With regard to the fashions of ladies' boots and shoes in the United States, since the American revolution, we have closely followed the examples set for us by the ladies of Paris and London. Many families still preserve as relics the high-heeled shoes worn by their female ancestors, previous to the American revolution. The levelling spirit of the French revolution, seems to have reached even to ladies' shoes; for we find that about 1790, the high heel was dispensed with, and shoes without heels were introduced. We have heard ladies of the olden time, say that it was hard to *come down* in this manner all at once; the effort to walk with no support to their heels was even painful, and our grandmothers were compelled for a long time to do penance to the tyrant fashion on tiptoe. Gradually, however, each lady found her own level, and succeeding generations, having never known the dangerous elevation of their predecessors, have found less difficulty in complying with the varying mandates of the goddess of *haut-ton*.

William G. Hooker, Esq., of New Haven, Connecticut, has collected between four and five hundred varieties of shoes, embracing the fashions for about two centuries in England and the United States.

To return to the fashions for gentlemen's boots. The Jefferson boot, which was introduced at about

the time when Mr. Jefferson came into the presidency (in 1801), and which that gentleman was himself fond of wearing, was laced up in front, as high as the ankles, in some instances perhaps higher; it was about this time that pantaloons were introduced into this country from France, and became fashionable.

The laced boot, which was laced up at the side, came in fashion soon after the Jefferson boot, but the inconvenience of lacing, prevented it from being generally adopted.

The snow-shoe, worn in Canada and other cold countries, is formed of a framework of wood, strongly interlaced with thongs of leather. It is used by travellers and hunters to prevent their sink-

13

ing into the snow, in their progress from place to place. It causes great pain to the wearer until after considerable practice in the use of it.

The Indian moccasin was the boot or shoe worn by the aborigines of America, before and after the settlement of this country by Europeans. It was made of deerskin, tanned by a mode peculiar to the Indians, and smoked; ornamented with beads or porcupines' quills or feathers, and worn without soles.

CHAPTER VIII.

BIOGRAPHICAL SKETCHES OF EMINENT SHOEMAKERS.

FROM the numerous instances on record, of individuals who have belonged to the "gentle craft" (by which name those who have learned the art of shoemaking are designated), and who by their talents have acquired distinction and eminence among their fellow-men, as statesmen, patriots, scholars, poets, or professional men, we select the following as interesting, and appropriate to this work.

ROGER SHERMAN.

"The self-taught Sherman urged his reasons clear."
. . *Humphrey's Poems.*

AMONG the illustrious characters whose names are inscribed upon the brightest record that adorns the annals of America, few possessed more solid attainments than Roger Sherman. He belonged to that class of statesmen who seek rather to convince the reason, than to triumph over the passions of men. The vigor of his mind appeared more conspicuous in the plain and simple manner in which it was elicited, than if it had been ornamented with all the beauties of elocution. But the energy of his address was not diminished by the absence of fanciful diction, nor the solidity of his views less admired because his feelings were partially suppressed. Without indulging in those brilliant bursts of oratory which please and sparkle for a moment, his impressive manner displayed ideas founded upon calm deliberation, and a clear perception of the justice of his cause. By a uniform and dispassionate course, he attained extensive influence in the councils of his country, and attracted the admiration and esteem of his compatriots. It has been said of him that he seldom failed to procure the adoption of any measure which he advocated, and which he considered essential to the public good.

Captain John Sherman, the ancestor of the subject of this sketch, emigrated to Massachusetts from Dedham, in England, about the year 1635.

William, the. father of Roger Sherman, was a farmer in moderate circumstances, and resided at Newton, Massachusetts, where the latter was born, April 19, 1721. The family removed to Stoughton, in the same state, in 1723.

There is a striking analogy between the early lives and self-promotion of Mr. Sherman and of Doctor Franklin. Surmounting difficulties which to common minds would have been insuperable, they gradually ascended from the humbler walks of life, to a prominent station among men. Of the childhood and early youth of Sherman, little is known. He received no other education than the ordinary country schools in Massachusetts at that period afforded. He was neither assisted by a public education, nor private tuition. All the valuable attainments which he exhibited in his future career, were the result of his own vigorous efforts. By his ardent thirst for knowledge, and his indefatigable industry, he attained a very commendable acquaintance with general science, the system of logic, geography, mathematics; the general principles of philosophy, history, theology; and particularly law and politics. He was early apprenticed to a *shoemaker*, and pursued that occupation until he was twenty-two years of age. He was accustomed to sit at his work with a book before him, devoting every moment that his eyes could be spared .from the occupation in which he was engaged.

Mr. Sherman was not one of those to whom the retrospect of past life was. unpleasant. During the revolutionary war, he was placed on a commit-

13*

tee of Congress, to examine certain army accounts, among which was a contract for the supply of shoes. He informed the committee that the public had been defrauded, and that the charges were exorbitant, which he proved by specifying the cost of the leather and other materials, and of the workmanship. The minuteness with which this was done, exciting some surprise, he informed the committee that he was by trade a shoemaker, and knew the value of every article.

The care of a numerous family of brothers and sisters, devolved on Mr. Sherman at the age of nineteen, on the death of his father, in 1741. He kindly provided for his mother, and assisted two brothers, afterward clergymen, to obtain an education.

He removed in 1743 to New Milford, Connecticut, travelling on foot, and carrying his shoemaker's tools upon his back. Soon after this, he relinquished his trade, and became the partner of an elder brother, a country merchant at New Milford, which connexion he continued until his admission to the bar in 1754. He was appointed surveyor of lands for the county where he resided in 1745. Astronomical calculations of as early date as 1748, have been found among his papers. They were made by him for an almanac, then published in

New York, and which he continued to supply for several successive years.

About this time, a lawyer whom he had occasion to consult on business, advised him to devote his attention to the study of the law. This counsel his circumstances did not permit him at once to follow, but the intimation he then received, that his mind was fitted for higher pursuits, no doubt induced him to devote his leisure moments to those studies which led him to honor and distinguished usefulness. Having acquired a competent knowledge of the law, he was admitted to practice in 1754. In the following year he was appointed a justice of the peace; he was also chosen a representative in the legislature, and a deacon in the church. Removing to New Haven in 1761, he was, in 1766, chosen an assistant or member of the upper house of the colonial legislature. The same year he was appointed a judge of the superior court of Connecticut, which office he held for 23 years, as he did that of assistant 19 years. His legal opinions were received with great deference by the profession, and their correctness was generally acknowledged.

Mr. Sherman took an early and active part in our revolutionary struggle, and in 1774 was chosen delegate to the first continental congress. Of that body and the federal congress, he continued a member for the long period of 19 years, till his death in 1793. In June, 1776, he was appointed on the committee with Jefferson, Adams, Franklin, and R. R. Livingston, to prepare the declaration of independence, of which instrument, when reported, and adopted by congress, he was one of the signers. John Adams said of Mr. Sherman, that he was "one of the soundest and strongest pillars of the revolution." While he was performing indefatigable labors in Congress, he devoted unremitting attention to duties at home. During the war he was a member of the governor's council of safety.

In 1784, Mr. Sherman was elected mayor of the city of New Haven. About the same time he was one of a committee of two, appointed by the legislature of Connecticut, to revise the laws of the state. In 1787, he was chosen, in conjunction with William Samuel Johnson, and Oliver Ellsworth, a delegate to the national convention, to frame the constitution of the United States. In that body Mr. Sherman bore a conspicuous part, in debate and on committees. Having signed the constitution, as adopted, his exertions in procuring the ratification in Connecticut, were highly important and successful. He published a series of papers, under the signature of "citizen," which materially in-

fluenced the public mind in favor of its adoption.
After the ratification of the constitution, he was
immediately elected by the people, as one of their
representatives in congress. Though approaching
the seventieth year of his age, he yet took a prominent part in the great topics of discussion which
came before the first congress. He zealously co-
operated with Washington, Hamilton, and others
of the same school of politics, in organizing the
government under the constitution. In 1791,
a vacancy having occurred in the senate of the
United States, Mr. Sherman was elected to fill that
elevated station, in which he continued until his
death, on the 23d of July, 1793, when he was gathered to his fathers, in the seventy third year of his
age. He died in full possession of all his powers,
both of mind and body.

"The legacy which Mr. Sherman has bequeathed
to his countrymen," says Professor Edwards, "is
indeed invaluable. The Romans never ceased to
mention with inexpressible gratitude, the heroism,
magnanimity, contentment, disinterestedness, and
noble public services of him who was called from
the plough to the dictator's chair. His example
was a light to all subsequent ages. So among the
galaxy of great men who shine along the paths of
our past history, we can scarcely refer to one, save

Washington, whose glory will be more steady and unfading than that of Roger Sherman."

In regard to worldly circumstances, Mr. Sherman was very happily situated. Beginning life without the aid of patrimonial wealth, or powerful connexions, he, by his industry and skilful management, always lived in a comfortable manner, and his property was gradually increasing. He was never grasping nor avaricious, but liberal in feeling, and in proportion to his means, liberal in acts of beneficence and hospitality. His manner of living was in accordance with the strictest republican simplicity.

In his person, Mr. Sherman was considerably above the common stature; his form was erect and well-proportioned; his complexion very fair, and his countenance manly and agreeable, indicating mildness, benignity, and decision. He did not neg- lect those smaller matters, without the observance of which a high station can not be sustained with propriety and dignity. In his dress he was plain, but remarkably neat; and in his treatment of men of every class, he was universally affable and obli- ging. In the private relations of husband, father, and friend, he was uniformly affectionate, faithful, and constant.

As a theologian, Mr. Sherman was capable of

conversing on the most important subjects, with reputation to himself, and improvement to others. As an avowed professor of religion, he did not hesitate to appear openly in its defence, and maintain the doctrines of Christianity. Among his correspondents were Dr. Jonathan Edwards, Dr. Hopkins, Dr. Trumbull, President Dickinson, President Witherspoon, Doctor Johnson of Connecticut, and many others.

DANIEL SHEFFEY.

THIS gentleman, one of the most distinguished members of the bar in the state of Virginia, a district of which he represented in Congress for eight years, namely, from 1809 to 1817, was in early life a shoemaker. His colleague, John Randolph of Roanoke, once alluded to the fact in debate, in his usual sarcastic mode, to which Mr. Sheffey retorted by acknowledging the truth of the allusion, and saying in substance: " The difference, sir, between the gentleman and myself, is this: that if his lot had been cast like mine, in early life, instead of rising by industry, enterprise, and study, above his calling, and occupying a seat on this floor, with which each of us is now honored by our constituents, he would at this time have been still engaged at his last on the workbench."

Mr. Sheffey was a conspicuous member of congress, during the four terms in which he served in the house, able in debate, and respected as a man of genius and good judgment. In politics he was attached to the federal party, and opposed to the declaration of war with Great Britain, and other measures of Mr. Madison's administration. On returning from congress, two years after the conclusion of the war, he applied himself to the practice of his profession as a lawyer, sustaining a high rank among the members of the bar in the ancient dominion. On his death, in December, 1830, the courts of Virginia, and others, united in public demonstrations of respect to his memory, as a man of genius, a distingushed counsellor, and an eminent and useful citizen. The records of debates in congress, bear ample testimony to his talents as a statesman and orator, among the able men with whom he was associated in the councils of the nation.

GIDEON LEE.

AMONG the many enterprising sons of New England, who have risen from humble life, and distinguished themselves by their industry and talents, the name of Gideon Lee stands conspicuous. Self-educated, and emphatically self-made, he rose to influence and distinction by the practice of those virtues which secure the respect and confidence of mankind. He rose from poverty and obscurity, to occupy, and worthily to fill, the most honorable situations in the gift of his fellow-citizens, and, by a long life of great public and private usefulness, distinguished for honesty, industry, sobriety, benevolence—and beyond this, evincing an enthusiasm in the cause of education, of the moral and intellectual culture of the people—entitled himself to be ranked as a patriot and public benefactor.

Gideon Lee was born in the town of Amherst, in the state of Massachusetts, on the 27th of April, 1778. He lost his father when quite a child, and was left to the care of his mother, of whom he always spoke in terms of the warmest affection. After his father's death, he went to reside with an uncle, a farmer, in whose service he discharged the humble duties of looking after the cattle, and was employed in such other occupations as were suitable to his strength and age.

After remaining some time under the care, and in the employment of his uncle, he was apprenticed to the tanning and shoemaking business, it being then the practice to conduct both branches by the same person, working at the former in the summer, and at the latter during the winter months.

14

For the tanning department, however, he always retained the strongest partiality. Up to this period, his opportunities for acquiring knowledge were extremely limited: a few weeks' schooling during the winter, and such books as accidentally fell in his way, were all the means vouchsafed to him. After learning his trade, or trades, he commenced business on his own account, in the town of Worthington, Massachusetts, and, by his industry and strict attention to it, won the regard and confidence of his neighbors. He was enabled to obtain credit for the purchase of leather, which he manufactured into shoes; always paying promptly for it at the period he had agreed. The first hundred dollars he earned, and that he could honestly call his own, he appropriated to educating himself at the Westfield academy. When that sum was exhausted, he again betook himself to his trade. His diligence and application were remarkable; sixteen hours out of the twenty-four, he usually devoted to labor.

After prosecuting his business for some time alone, he formed a partnership in trade with a friend; subsequently they were burned out, and Mr. Lee lost what little property he had accumulated. He then dissolved with his partner, and removed to the city of New York. But before establishing himself permanently in the city, he made

a voyage to St. Mary's, Georgia, taking with him a
small adventure in leather. The adventure not
proving a profitable one, he returned to New York,
after remaining one winter at the south. The vessel in which he took passage being wrecked off
Cape Fear, he made the journey to New York, in
company with a Yankee friend, on foot. In one
instance on this pedestrian journey, his money being
exhausted, he chopped wood for a farmer, to pay
for his food and lodging.

About the year 1807, Mr. Lee commenced business as a leather-dealer, in a small building in
Ferry street, New York. Being appointed agent
for an extensive tanning establishment in Massachusetts, called the "Hampshire Leather Manufactory,"
he laid the foundation in the city of New York,
for a trade in a branch of domestic industry, which
speedily rivalled any in the other Atlantic cities.
His prudence, punctuality, and economy, enabled
him to accumulate means for enlarging his business; and but for feeble health, the future to him
was a bright path of success. In this business,
namely, the selling of leather on commission, he
continued for about thirty years, until his final retirement from mercantile pursuits.

In the fall of 1822, Mr. Lee was elected a member of assembly, in the New York legislature,

where he distinguished himself by his close application to the business of the house, being seldom
out of his place while it was in session.   In 1833,
he was elected by the common council of New
York, mayor of that city, having previously served
several years in the capacity of alderman.   While
discharging the duties of the mayoralty, he with-
drew entirely from active participation in managing
the business of his mercantile house, and devoted
all his time and abilities to the public service.   It
was a maxim with him, that "whatever was worth
doing at all was worth doing well."   In his communications to the common council, he never failed
on suitable occasions to call their attention to the
subject of public education ;—it was a theme on
which he never tired.

In 1834, an alteration in the charter, made the
office of mayor of New York elective by the people.   A nomination was offered to Mr. Lee, but he
declined a re-election, finding it necessary to return
to his mercantile business.   From this period, he
contemplated retiring from commercial pursuits,
and accordingly commenced winding up the affairs
of his long-established concern in Ferry street.   It
was not, however, until the fall of 1836, that he
felt himself in a situation to retire from its management.

He then again entered for a short period into
public life, and represented the city of New York
in the twenty-fourth congress, where he was distinguished for his business habits, for his close attention to the interests of his constituents, and, we
might also say, for making short speeches. Dis-
daining the arts of the demagogue, he made no
efforts to acquire an ephemeral popularity in the
usual modes, and was consequently not re-elected
to congress. His political life may be said to have
ended with the termination of the session of congress, in March, 1837, with an exception. He was
in 1840, chosen a member of the electoral college
of New York, for choosing the president and vice-
president of the United States.

In politics Mr. Lee was a democratic republican,
and supported the administrations of Jefferson,
Madison, Monroe, and Jackson. Disapproving,
however, of the measures of Mr. Van Buren's administration, he became what was called a " conserv-
ative," acting with the whigs after the year 1837,
and was chosen by that party one of the electoral
college, which gave the vote of the state to General
Harrison, as president of the United States.

Shortly after retiring from congress, Mr. Lee
removed to the village of Geneva, in Ontario county, New York, where he had purchased a beautiful

14*

estate; and in improving and adorning it, and in
the education of his children, he contemplated
spending the remainder of his days. He had, however, but barely commenced, as he expressed it,
"winding up his end of life," in the manner he had
so long and ardently desired, when death removed
him from his labors. He was seized with bilious
fever, accompanied by neuralgia, early in July,
1841, and on the 21st of August succeeding, was
gathered to his fathers, in the sixty-fourth year of
his age, leaving to his family an ample fortune, the
honest fruits of a well-spent life.

Of one who thus lived, it will create no surprise
to be informed that he was prepared to die. Death
did not find him a reluctant or unwilling voyager to
his dark domains. At his beckoning he laid down
his plans and cares with cheerfulness and pious
resignation to the divine will, and sunk with calm
dignity to his last repose, with a grateful heart for
all the blessings and mercies he had experienced.
He died full of faith and hope in the promises of
his Redeemer.

"The lamp of life of such men," says his friend
and biographer, "can not be extinguished without
casting around a gloom; their absence from society
creates a void that must be ever felt. They may
leave no blazing reputation to dazzle or astonish,

but they leave one that distributes its invigorating influence, wherever virtue has a friend, or philanthropy an advocate."*

SAMUEL DREW.

THOSE individuals who have raised themselves from obscurity to distinction, always attract our notice; but when that distinction has been attained in spite of obstacles apparently insurmountable, they become the especial objects of our curiosity. This feeling is not only laudable but beneficial. Curiosity leads to knowledge; knowledge causes admiration; and admiration becomes an incentive to honorable effort. It is this which gives to biography its value; and of few persons can the biography be more instructive than that of the subject of this sketch.

Samuel Drew was born on the third of March, 1765, near St. Austell, in the county of Cornwall, England. He was the second son of four children. His parents were poor, but pious. His father, who earned a bare subsistence for himself and family by his daily labor as a husbandman, was a convert to methodism under the preaching of John Wesley, whose society he joined in early life. His mother,

* Merchants' Magazine.

whom he had the misfortune to lose before he was ten years old, was a decidedly religious woman, and of strong intellectual powers. Of her memory he always spoke with reverence and affection; and the pious lessons which, in his infancy, he learned from her, were never forgotten.

The poverty of his parents prevented him from receiving many of the advantages of an early education. He however learned to form the letters of the alphabet, previous to his mother's death, but at eight years of age, he was taken from school, and sent to work at a mill near his father's cottage, where tinners refined their ore. His wages were at first three halfpence, and were afterward advanced to two pence per day. When rather more than ten years old, his father bound him an apprentice for nine years, to a shoemaker, in an adjoining parish.

During his apprenticeship, Drew had occasional access to a little publication called the "Weekly Entertainer," which was then extensively circulated in the west of England, and contained many tales and narratives which interested him. Into the narratives of adventures connected with the war of the American revolution, he entered with all the zeal of a partisan on the side of the Americans. He felt a strong desire to join himself to a privateer, but having no money and few clothes, the idea and scheme were vain. Besides these periodicals, he read but little, and nearly lost the art of writing. The treatment he received while an apprentice, being such as his disposition could not brook, he left his master when about seventeen, and refused to return. His father compounded for the residue of the term, and procured him employment, and further instruction in his business, at Millbrook, near Plymouth, in which place and neighborhood he continued about three years. In 1785, when about twenty years of age, he went to St. Austell, to conduct the shoemaking business for a person who was by trade a saddler, and had acquired some knowledge of book-binding. With this employer he continued about two years, and then commenced business as a shoemaker in that town, on his own account. A miller with whom he was acquainted, lent him five pounds, as capital in trade, fourteen shillings being the total of his own cash, his thirst for knowledge having induced him to lay out in books such money as he could save from his earnings as a journeyman. He joined the methodist society in 1785, soon after becoming the subject of religious impressions, under the preaching of the celebrated Adam Clarke, with whom he soon afterward became acquainted; and the friendship and intimacy of that distingushed divine, Mr. Drew continued to enjoy through life. By no one were the peculiar and extraordinary talents developed by Mr. Drew, more fully appreciated than by his friend Doctor Clarke. Soon after joining the methodists, Mr. Drew's abilities were called into exercise; he was appointed to the charge of a class, and employed as a local preacher. In this field, except as a class-leader, which he resigned into other hands, he continued to labor until a few months before his decease.

The occasional perusal of books which were brought to the shop of his employer to be bound, awakened Mr. Drew to a consciousness of his own ignorance, and determined him to acquire knowledge. Every moment he could snatch from sleep and labor, was now devoted to the reading of such books as his limited finances placed within his reach. One of the difficulties which he had to encounter at this outset of his literary career, arose from his ignorance of the import of words. To overcome this, he found it necessary, while reading, to keep a dictionary constantly at hand. The process was tedious, but it was unavoidable; and difficulties lessened at every step.

A new world was now opened before him. All its paths were untried, and in what direction to push his inquiries, he was yet, undecided. Astronomy first attracted his attention; but to the pursuit of this, his ignorance of arithmetic and geometry was an insuperable obstacle. In history, to which his views were next directed, no proficiency could be made without extensive reading, and he had too little command of time and money for such a purpose. The religious bias which he had received, tended, however, to give a theological direction to his studies, and from the apparently accidental inspection of "Locke's Essay on the Human Understanding," he acquired a predilection for the higher exercises of the mind.

In April, 1791, Mr. Drew married, being then in a creditable way of business as a shoemaker. He was not yet an author, but had obtained a name for skill and integrity as a tradesman, and was held in respect by his neighbors. Doctor Franklin's "Way to Wealth," fell into his hands about the time he commenced business for himself. The pithy and excellent advice of "Poor Richard," in that work, instructed and delighted him. He placed it in a conspicuous situation in his chamber, and resolved to follow its maxims. Eighteen hours out of twenty-four, he regularly worked, and sometimes longer; for his friends gave him plenty of employment, but until the bills became due, he had no means of paying wages to a journeyman. He remarks: "I was indefatigable, and at the year's end, I had the satisfaction of paying the five pounds which had been so kindly lent me, and finding myself, with a tolerable stock of leather, clear of the world."

By unremitting industry, he at length surmounted such obstacles as were of a pecuniary nature. This enabled him to procure assistance in his labors, and thus afforded him some relaxation. Industry and rigid economy were still indispensable, but his ruling passion, the acquisition of knowledge, he was enabled to gratify in a limited degree, and for several years, every spare moment, and all the hours he could snatch from sleep, were devoted to reading such books as he could procure.

Referring to this period of his life, in conversation with a friend, Mr. Drew said: "I once had a very great desire for the study of astronomy, for I thought it suitable to the genius of my mind, and I think so still; but then—

> "Chill penury repressed the noble rage,
> And froze the genial current of the soul."

Dangers and difficulties I did not fear, while I could bring the powers of my mind to bear upon them, and force myself a passage. To metaphysics I then applied myself, and became what the world and my good friend Doctor Clarke call "a metaphysician."

As he could devote but little time to the acquisition of knowledge, every moment was fully occupied. "Drive thy business—do not let thy business drive thee," was one of those maxims of Dr. Franklin, to which Mr. Drew adhered; and his example shows that literature may be cultivated, and piety pursued, without prejudice to our worldly interests.

"During several years," he observes, "all my leisure hours were devoted to reading or scribbling; but I do not recollect that it ever interrupted my business, though it frequently broke in upon my rest. On my labor depended my livelihood; literary pursuits were only my amusement. The man who *makes shoes* is sure of his wages—the man who writes a book is never sure of anything."

Mr. Drew's first attempts at composition, like those of most young essayists in the paths of literature, were metrical. The earliest known effort of his muse, was a poetical epistle to his sister, and the next an elegy on the death of his brother. These were followed by several short poetical pieces, none of which have been preserved. He left in manuscript a metrical piece containing about 1200 lines, entitled "Reflections on St. Austell

15

Churchyard," dated August, 1792. It is written in the heroic stanza, and has many excellent couplets, but is too defective in grammar and versification, to endure the test of criticism. The major part is argumentative—not unlike "Pope's Essay on Man," upon which, possibly, it was modelled: and several of the arguments tend to prove that the soul is immaterial, and therefore immortal. This poetical composition is apparently the embryo of Mr. Drew's applauded "Treatise on the Human Soul." From the year 1792, when this poem was written, until the commencement of his "Essay on the Soul, in 1798, no particular circumstance of his literary life is on record.

His own description of his mode of study at this period of his life is as follows : "During my literary pursuits, I regularly and constantly attend on my business, and do not recollect that one customer was ever disappointed through these means. My mode of writing and study may have in them perhaps something peculiar. Immersed in the common concerns of life, I endeavor to lift my thoughts to objects more sublime than those with which I am surrounded; and while attending to my trade, I sometimes catch the fibres of an argument, which I endeavor to note, and keep a pen and ink by me for that purpose. In this state, what I can collect

through the day, remains on any paper which I
have at hand, till the business of the day is de-
spatched, and my shop shut, when, in the midst of
my family, I endeavor to analyze, in the evening,
such thoughts as had crossed my mind during the
day. I have no study—I have no retirement—I
write amid the cries and cradles of my children;
and frequently, when I review what I have written,
endeavor to cultivate 'the art to blot.' Such are
the methods which I have pursued, and such the
disadvantages under which I write."

The circumstances which led to his becoming an
author, are these: A young gentleman with whom
he was intimate, by profession a surgeon, put into
his hands the first part of Paine's Age of Reason,
thinking to bring him over to the principles of infi-
delity. The sophistry of Paine's book, Mr. Drew
readily detected; and committing his thoughts to
writing in the form of notes, by the advice of two
methodist preachers, to whom he showed them, he
was induced to publish them in a pamphlet entitled,
" Remarks on Paine's Age of Reason," in Septem-
ber, 1799. This little work was favorably received
by the public; and it procured for its author, the
steady friendship of the Rev. John Whitaker, a
clergyman of high literary reputation.

Upon the Remarks on Paine's Age of Reason,

which first brought Mr. Drew before the public as
an author, a writer in the Anti-Jacobin Review, of
April, 1801, observes, " We here see a shoemaker
of St. Austell, encountering a staymaker of Deal,
with the same weapons of unlettered reason, tem-
pered, indeed, from the armory of God, yet deriv-
ing their principal power from the native vigor of
the arm that wields them. Samuel Drew, however,
is greatly superior to Thomas Paine, in the just-
ness of his remarks, in the forcibleness of his arguments, and in the pointedness of his refutations."
Mr. Drew had the satisfaction of knowing, that his
" Remarks" were the means of leading the young
man who put the Age of Reason into his hands,
to renounce his deistical principles, and to embrace,
with full conviction the doctrines of Christianity.
The Remarks on Paine, having been several years
out of print, were republished, in duodecimo, with
the author's corrections and additions, in 1820.

The appearance in 1802, of the " Essay on the
Immateriality and Immortality of the Soul," to
which Mr. Drew is chiefly indebted for his reputation as a metaphysician, brought him into honorable notice beyond his native county. This
book was dedicated to the Rev. John Whitaker,
whose patronage had, in a great measure, drawn
him forth from obscurity. The work has since

gone through several editions in England and America, and has been translated into the French language, and published in France.

Encouraged by the favorable reception of this work by the public, Mr. Drew continued his literary labors. His next important attempt in metaphysics, was an investigation of the evidences of a general resurrection. From this investigation, the subject of personal identity was inseparable; and on these topics he recorded his thoughts till the close of the year 1805. At that time he took a survey of his work, but was so much dissatisfied with it, that he threw the whole aside as useless, and half resolved to touch it no more; nor did it appear in print (after being revised by the author) until 1809. It was then, like the Essay on the Soul, published by subscription, and the copyright sold to a London publisher. Fifteen hundred copies were printed, and a second edition appeared in 1822. This work on the Resurrection has also been republished in the United States.

In 1805, Mr. Drew entered into an engagement with the late Doctor Thomas Cope, one of the founders of the Wesleyan methodist missions, to assist him in his literary labors, which wholly detached him from the pursuits of trade. From this time literature became his occupation. About two years

15*

previously to this, Mr. Drew had undertaken, in a course of familiar lectures, to instruct a class of young persons and adults, in English grammar and composition. A similar course of lectures, with the addition of geography and astronomy, was delivered by him, in 1811.

Mr. Drew's various works introduced to the notice, and procured for him the friendship, of several distinguished individuals. His intimacy with Doctor Adam Clarke continued through many years, and with him he long maintained a correspondence. In 1819, at the recommendation of Doctor Clarke, Mr. Drew was engaged as editor of the Imperial Magazine. This led to his removal to Liverpool, and thence to London, where he continued to discharge the duties of editor until 1833. Besides the editorship of the Magazine, he had the superintendence of all the works issued from the Caxton press.

In consequence of symptoms of rapidly-declining health, Mr. Drew left London for his native place in Cornwall, in March, 1833, where he died on the 29th of the same month, at the age of sixty-eight.

Besides the works already mentioned, Mr, Drew was the author of a life of his friend Doctor Coke, a History of Cornwall, Essays on the Divinity of

Christ and the Necessity of his Atonement, and several other religious works, of a high character. He was also associated with Doctor Coke in writing several important works bearing the name of Doctor Coke as author.

Mr. Drew was an acute reasoner and a close and laborious thinker. He always discovered where truth lay; sophistry rarely escaped his detection; and to his habit of persevering and patient investigation, we are indebted for his most elaborate and convincing arguments. He has been called the "*Locke of the nineteenth century.*"

Those who would estimate Mr. Drew's mental powers, should bear in mind the difficulties which he surmounted. From education he derived no assistance. His youth was passed in ignorance and poverty; and he was twenty years of age, before he began to read or to think. Yet before he attained the meridian of life he had accumulated a vast fund of knowledge. Nor was that knowledge limited to the subjects on which he wrote; it extended to various branches of science; and there were few topics of speculative philosophy, with which he was unacquainted.

ROBERT BLOOMFIELD.

THE preceding sketches record the names of individuals who have severally distinguished themselves in statesmanship, patriotism, philanthropy,
eloquence, and metaphysics. It is pleasing to add
to our list, one whose name is familiar as an English pastoral poet.

Robert Bloomfield was born at the village of
Honington, Suffolk county, England, December 3,
1766, and was the youngest of six children. His
father, George Bloomfield, was a tailor, and died
before his youngest son was a year old, leaving
his widow to obtain a scanty subsistence for herself and family, by teaching a small school, in
which Robert was taught to read. Two or three
months' instruction in writing was all the scholastic
accomplishment that he ever obtained. At the age
of eleven he was hired in the neighborhood as a
farmer's boy, but being found too feeble for agri-
cultural labor, he was placed with an elder brother
in London, to learn the trade of a shoemaker.

"In the garret where five of us worked," his
brother writes, "I received little Robert. As we
were all single men, lodgers at a shilling per week
each, our beds were coarse, and all things far from
being clean and snug. Robert was our man to

fetch all things to hand. At noon he fetched our dinner from the cook's shop; and any of our fellow-workmen, that wanted to have anything brought in, would send him, and assist in his work, and teach him as a recompense for his trouble.

"Every day when the boy from the public house came for the pewter-pots, and to hear what porter was wanted, he always brought the yesterday's newspaper. The reading of the paper we had been used to take by turns; but after Robert came, he mostly read for us, because his time was of least value. He frequently met with words that he was unacquainted with; of this he often complained. I bought a small dictionary for him. By the help of this, he in a little time could read and comprehend the long and beautiful speeches of Burke, Fox, and North."

When about sixteen years of age, Robert had an opportunity to read Thomson's "Seasons"—which was a favorite book with him—Milton's "Paradise Lost," and a few novels. Soon afterward, he left the employment of his brother, and spent a few months in his native county, with the farmer with whom he had formerly lived; and here free from the smoke and noise of London, he imbibed that love of rural simplicity and innocence, which he afterward displayed in his poems.

Returning to his trade of shoemaker in London, he was bound to Mr. John Dudbridge, and after he was of age, worked as journeyman for Davies, ladies' shoemaker. In a garret, while at work with six or seven others, he composed his beautiful rural poem, "The Farmer's Boy." A great part of this poem was composed by him, without committing one line to paper. When it was thus prepared, he said, "I had nothing to do but to write it down." By this mode of composition, he studied and completed his "Farmer's Boy," in a garret, among his fellow-workmen, without their ever suspecting or knowing anything of the matter. That the reader may judge of the merits of this poem, we quote the invocation:—

"O come, blest spirit! whatsoe'er thou art,
 Thou kindling warmth that hoverest round my heart,
 Sweet inmate, hail! thou source of sterling joy,
 That poverty itself can not destroy,
 Be thou my muse; and faithful still to me,
 Retrace the paths of wild obscurity.
 No deeds of arms, my humble lines rehearse,
 No *Alpine* wonders thunder through my verse,
 The roaring cataract, the snow-topt hill,
 Inspiring awe, till breath itself stands still;
 Nature's sublimer scenes ne'er charmed mine eyes,
 Nor science led me through the boundless skies,
 From meaner objects far, my raptures flow,
 O point these raptures! bid my bosom glow!

And lead my soul to ecstasies of praise,
For all the blessings of my infant days,
Bear me through regions where gay fancy dwells,
But mould to Truth's fair form, what memory tells."

The manuscript of "the Farmer's Boy," after being offered to and refused by several London publishers, was printed under the patronage of Capel Lofft, Esq., in 1800; and the admiration it produced was so great, that within three years after its publication, more than 26,000 copies were sold. The appearance of such refinement of taste and sentiment in the person of an indigent artisan, elicited general applause. An edition was published in the following year at Leipsic. It was also translated into French, Italian, and Latin.

The fame of Bloomfield was further increased by the subsequent publication of "Rural Tales, Ballads, and Songs," "Good Tidings, or News from the Farm," "Wild Flowers," and "Banks of the Wye." He was kindly noticed by the duke of Grafton, by whom he was appointed to a situation in the seal office; but suffering from constitutional ill-health, he returned to his trade of ladies' shoemaker, to which, being an amateur in music, he added the employment of making Æolian harps. A pension of a shilling a day was still allowed him by the duke, yet having now, besides a wife and children, undertaken to support several other members of his family, he became involved in difficulties, and being habitually in bad health, he retired to Shefford in Bedfordshire, where, in 1816, a subscription, headed by the duke of Norfolk, and other noblemen, was instituted by the friendship of Sir Edgerton Brydges, for the relief of his embarrassments. Great anxiety of mind, occasioned by accumulated misfortunes and losses, with violent incessant headaches, a morbid nervous irritability, and loss of memory, reduced him at last to a condition little short of insanity. He died at Shefford, August 19, 1823, at the age of fifty-seven, leaving a widow and four children, and debts to the amount of two hundred pounds sterling, which sum was raised by subscription among his benevolent friends and admirers.

The works of Bloomfield have been published in two volumes duodecimo. The author's amiable disposition and benevolence pervade the whole of his compositions. There is an artless simplicity, a virtuous rectitude of sentiment, an exquisite sensibility to the beautiful, which can not fail to gratify every one who respects moral excellence, and loves the delightful scenes of English country life.

NATHANIEL BLOOMFIELD.

NATHANIEL BLOOMFIELD, brother of the foregoing, was likewise a shoemaker and a poet; and
although "Nathan's" name does not sound the most
poetical in Lord Byron's line, yet we believe many
of our readers would admire some of his pieces
before some of the noble poet's, for reasons extrin-
sic of execution or subject. His stanzas on the
Enclosure of Honnington Green, quoted by Kirke
White in his essays, would be admired by most
readers. We transcribe some of the remarks
of the amiable critic, including a quotation that
will give an idea of Mr. Bloomfield's poetic abilities, whose writings are not so generally known as
those of his brother.

"Had Mr. N. Bloomfield," says Henry Kirke
White, "made his appearance in the horizon of
letters prior to his brother, he would undoubtedly
have been considered as a meteor of uncommon at-
traction; the critics would have admired, because
it was the fashion to admire. But it is to be apprehended that our countrymen become inured to phe-
nomena—it is to be apprehended that the frivolity
of the age can not endure a repetition of the uncommon—that it will no longer be the rage to pat-
ronize indigent merit—that the *beau monde* will

16

therefore neglect, and that, by a necessary consequence, the critics will sneer!

"Nevertheless, sooner or later, merit will meet
with its reward; and though the popularity of Mr.
Bloomfield may be delayed, he *must*, at one time or
other, receive the meed due to its deserts. Posterity will judge impartially; and if bold and vivid
images, and original conceptions, luminously displayed, and judiciously apposed, have any claim to
the regard of mankind, the name of Nathaniel
Bloomfield will not be without its high and appropriate honors.

"That Mr. N. Bloomfield's poems display acute-
ness of remark, and delicacy of sentiment, combined with much strength, and considerable *selec-
tion* of diction, few will deny. The Pæan to Gun-
powder would alone prove both his power of language, and the fertility of his imagination; and the
following extract presents him to us in the still
higher character of a bold and vivid *painter*. Describing the field after a battle, he says,

'Now here and there, about the horrid field,
Striding across the dying and the dead,
Stalks up a man, by strength superior,
Or skill and prowess in the arduous fight
Preserved alive: — fainting he looks around;
Fearing pursuit — not caring to pursue.
The supplicating voice of bitterest moans,

> Contortions of excruciating pain,
> The shriek of torture, and the groan of death,
> Surround him; — and as night her mantle spreads,
> To veil the horrors of the mourning field,
> With cautious step shaping his devious way,
> He seeks a covert where to hide and rest:
> At every leaf that rustles in the breeze
> Starting, he grasps his sword; and every nerve
> Is ready strained for combat or for flight.'

" If Mr. Bloomfield had written nothing besides the Elegy on the Enclosure of Honnington Green, he would have had a right to be considered as a poet of no mean excellence. There is a sweet and tender melancholy pervading the elegiac ballad efforts of Mr. Bloomfield, which has the most indescribable effects on the heart. Were the versification a little more polished, in some instances, they would be read with unmixed delight."

WILLIAM GIFFORD.

WILLIAM GIFFORD was born in 1755, at Ashburton, in Devonshire, England, and for several years led the miserable kind of life which is common among the children of a drunken and reckless father. His father died when only forty years of age, leaving his wife with two children, the youngest little more than eight months old, and no available means for their support. In about a year afterward his wife followed, and thus was William, at the age of thirteen, and his infant brother, thrown upon the world in an utterly destitute condition.

The parish workhouse now received the younger of the orphans, and William was taken home to the house of a person named Carlile, his godfather, who, whatever might have been his kindness in this respect, had at least taken care of his own interests, by seizing on every article left by the widow Gifford, on pretence of repaying himself for money which he had advanced to her, in her greatest necessities. The only benefit derived by William from this removal was a little education; as Carlile sent him to school, where he acquired the elements of instruction. His chief proficiency, as he tells us, was in arithmetic; but he was not suffered to make much progress in his studies, for, grudging the expense, his patron took him from school, with the object of making him a ploughboy. To the plough he would accordingly have gone, but for a weakness in his chest, the result of an accident some years before. It was now proposed to send him to a storehouse in Newfoundland; but the person who was to be benefited by his services declared him to be too small, and this plan was also dropped. "My godfather," says William, "had now humbler views for me, and I had little heart to re-

sist anything. He proposed to send me on board
one of the Torbay fishing-boats. I ventured, however, to remonstrate against this, and the matter
was compromised by my consenting to go on board
a coaster. A coaster was speedily found for me at
Brixham, and thither I went, when little more than
thirteen."

In this vessel he remained for nearly a year. "It
will be easily conceived," he remarks, "that my
life was a life of hardship. I was not only a 'ship-
boy on the high and giddy mast,' but also in the
cabin, where every menial office fell to my lot; yet
if I was restless and discontented, I can safely say
it was not so much on account of this, as of my
being precluded from all possibility of reading; as
my master did not possess, nor do I recollect seeing, during the whole time of my abode with him,
a single book of any description except the 'Coast-
ing Pilot.'"

While in this humble situation, however, and
seeming to himself almost an outcast from the
world, he was not forgotten. He had broken off
all connexion with Ashburton, where his godfather
lived; but "the women of Brixham," says he, "who
travelled to Ashburton twice a week with fish, and
who had known my parents, did not see me without kind concern running about the beach, in rag-

16*

ged jacket and trousers." They often mentioned him to their acquaintances at Ashburton; and the tale excited so much commiseration in the place, that his godfather at last found himself obliged to send for him home. At this time he wanted some months of fourteen. He proceeds with his own story as follows :—

"After the holydays, I returned to my darling pursuit—arithmetic. My progress was now so rapid, that in a few months I was at the head of the school, and qualified to assist my master (Mr. E. Furlong) on any extraordinary emergency. As he usually gave me a trifle on these occasions, it raised a thought in me, that, by engaging with him as a regular assistant, and undertaking the instruction of a few evening scholars, I might, with a little additional aid, be enabled to support myself. God knows my ideas of support at this time were of no very extravagant nature. I had, besides, another object in view. Mr. Hugh Smerdon (my first master) was now grown old and infirm; it seemed unlikely that he should hold out above three or four years; and I fondly flattered myself that, notwithstanding my youth, I might possibly be appointed to succeed him.

"I was in my fifteenth year when I built these castles. A storm, however, was collecting, which unexpectedly burst upon me, and swept them all away.

"On mentioning my little plan to Carlile, he treated it with the utmost contempt; and told me, in his turn, that as I had learned enough, and more than enough, at school, he must be considered as having fairly discharged his duty (so indeed he had); he added that he had been negotiating with his cousin, a shoemaker of some respectability who had liberally agreed to take me, without a fee, as an apprentice. I was so shocked at this intelligence, that I did not remonstrate, but went in sullenness and silence to my new master, to whom I was soon after bound, till I should attain the age of twenty-one.

"At this time," he continues, "I possessed but one book in the world: it was a treatise on algebra, given to me by a young woman, who had found it in a lodging-house. I considered it as a treasure; but it was a treasure locked up; for it supposed the reader to be well acquainted with simple equations, and I knew nothing of the matter. My master's son had purchased Fenning's Introduction: this was precisely what I wanted; but he carefully concealed it from me, and I was indebted to chance alone for stumbling upon his hiding-place. I sat up for the greatest part of sev-

eral nights successively, and, before he suspected
that his treatise was discovered, had completely
mastered it. I could now enter upon my own, and
that carried me pretty far into the science. This
was not done without difficulty. I had not a far-
thing on earth, nor a friend to give me one; pen,
ink, and paper, therefore, were for the most part
as completely out of my reach as a crown and scep-
tre. There was indeed a resource; but the utmost
caution and secresy were necessary in applying to
it. I beat out pieces of leather as smooth as possible, and wrote my problems on them with a
blunted awl; for the rest, my memory was tenacious,
and I could multiply and divide by it to a great extent."

Persevering under these untoward difficulties,
he at length obtained some alleviation of his poverty. Having attempted to write some verses, his
productions were received with applause, and
sometimes, he adds, "with favors more substantial:
little collections were now and then made, and I
have received sixpence in an evening. To one who
had long lived in the absolute want of money, such
a resource seemed a Peruvian mine. I furnished
myself by degrees with paper, &c., and what was
of more importance, with books of geometry, and
of the higher branches of algebra, which I cau-

tiously concealed. Poetry, even at this time, was no amusement of mine—it was subservient to other purposes; and I only had recourse to it when I wanted money for my mathematical pursuits."

Gifford's master having capriciously put a stop to these literary recreations, and taken away all his books and papers, he was greatly mortified, if not reduced to a state of despair. "I look back," he says, "on that part of my life which immediately followed this event, with little satisfaction: it was a period of gloom and savage unsociability. By degrees I sunk into a kind of corporeal torpor; or, if roused into activity by the spirit of youth, wasted the exertion in splenetic and vexatious tricks, which alienated the few acquaintances which compassion had yet left me."

Fortunately, this despondency in time gave way to a natural buoyancy of his disposition; some evidences of kindly feeling from those around him, tended a good deal to mitigate his recklessness; and especially as the term of his apprenticeship drew toward a close, his former aspirations and hopes began to return to him. Working with renewed diligence at his craft, he, at the end of six years, came under the notice of Mr. William Cookesley, and, struck with his talents, this benevolent person resolved on rescuing him from obscurity. "The plan," says Gifford, "that occurred to him was naturally that which had so often suggested itself to me. There were indeed several obstacles to be overcome. My handwriting was bad, and my language very incorrect; but nothing could slacken the zeal of his excellent man. He procured a few of my poor attempts at rhyme, dispersed them among his friends and acquaintance, and when my name was become somewhat familiar to them, set on foot a subscription for my relief. I still preserve the original paper; its title was not very magnificent, though it exceeded the most sanguine wishes of my heart. It ran thus: 'A subscription for purchasing the remainder of the time of William Gifford, and for enabling him to improve himself in writing and English grammar.' Few contributed more than five shillings, and none went beyond ten and sixpence; enough, however, was collected to free me from my apprenticeship, and to maintain me for a few months, during which I assiduously attended the Rev. Thomas Smerdon."

Pleased with the advances he made in this short period, it was agreed to maintain him at school for an entire year. "Such liberality," says Gifford, "was not lost upon me: I grew anxious to make the best return in my power, and I redoubled my diligence. Now that I am sunk into indolence, I look back with some degree of skepticism to the exertions of that period." In two years and two months from what he calls the day of his emancipation, he was pronounced by his master to be fit for the university; and a small office having been obtained for him, by Mr. Cookesley's exertions, at Oxford, he was entered of Exeter college, that gentleman undertaking to provide the additional means necessary to enable him to live till he should take his degree. Mr. Gifford's first patron died before his protegé had time to fulfil the good man's fond anticipations of his future celebrity; but he afterward found, in Lord Grosvenor, another much more able, though it was impossible that any other could have shown more zeal, to advance his interests.

Gifford was now on the way to fame, and he may be said to have ever afterward enjoyed a prosperous career. On the commencement of the " Quarterly Review," in 1809, he was appointed editor of that periodical, and under his management it attained a distinguished success. After a useful literary career, Mr. Gifford died in London on the 31st of December, 1826, in the seventy-first year of his age. Reversing the Latin proverb, it might be justly observed, that in him *a shoemaker happily went beyond his last.*

NOAH WORCESTER, D: D.

NOAH WORCESTER was born in 1758 at Hollis,
New Hampshire, where some of his ancestors had
been ministers; but his father was a farmer. In
early life he received very little education, and the
greater part of his time was consumed working
as a laborer in the fields. He afterward became a
soldier; but, horrified with the vices of that profession, and the slaughter which he saw take place
at Bunker's hill, he abandoned it for ever, and betook himself to farming. He now commenced a
course of self-instruction; and to lose no time
while so engaged, he employed himself in shoemaking. His diligence was unrelaxing. At the end
of his bench lay his books, pens, ink, and paper;
and to these he made frequent application. In this
way he acquired much useful learning; and a pamphlet which he wrote had the effect of recommending him to a body of ministers, by whom he was
advanced to the clerical profession.

In a short time an opening occurred for a preacher, in a small town in the neighborhood, and to this
he was promoted by universal consent; yet, in a
worldly sense, it was a poor promotion. His salary scantily supported life, being only two hundred
dollars, and as many could ill afford to pay their
proportion of even that small sum, he was accus-

tomed, as the time of collecting it drew nigh, to re-
linquish his claims, by giving to the poorer among
them receipts in full. The relief granted in this
way sometimes amounted to a fourth, or even a
third part of his salary. He was thus made to continue still dependent for his support in a great
measure on the labor of his hands, partly on the
farm, and partly in making shoes. But he was far
from fancying this scantiness of pay and necessity
of toil, any exemption from his obligation to do the
utmost for his people. On the contrary, he was
ready to engage in extra labor for them; and when
it happened, for example, as it sometimes did, that
the provision for a winter school failed, he threw
open the doors of his own house, invited the children into his study, and gave them his time and
care as assiduously as if he had been their regular-
ly-appointed teacher.

His short experience of soldiering, gave him, as
has been said, a horror of war, and against this
scourge he preached with untiring zeal. In 1814,
he gave vent to his whole soul, in a remarkable
tract, "A Solemn Review of the Custom of War,"
one of the most successful and efficient pamphlets
of any period. It has been translated into many
languages, and circulated extensively through the
world. It is one of the chief instruments by which

17

the opinions of society have been affected within
the present century.   The season of its publication
was favorable; the world was wearied with battles,
and longed for rest.   "Such was the impression
made by this work," says Dr. Channing, "that a
new association, called the 'Peace Society of Massachusetts,' was instituted in this place [Brighton,
Massachusetts, whither he had removed in 1813].
I well recollect the day of its formation in yonder
house, then the parsonage of this parish; and if
there was a happy man that day on earth, it was
the founder of this institution.   This society gave
birth to all the kindred ones in this country, and its
influence was felt abroad."   He conducted its periodical, which was commenced in 1819, and was
published quarterly for ten years.   It was almost
entirely written by himself, and is remarkable not
only for its beautiful moral tone, but for fertility
of resource and ingenuity of illustration.   He
wished it to be inscribed on his tombstone: "He
wrote the Friend of Peace."   Eight years after he
began to write the "Solemn Review," he declares
his belief that the subject of war had not been ab-
sent from his mind, when awake, an hour at a time,
during that whole period.   This concentration of
all the powers of an earnest and vigorous mind,
enabled him to produce a greater effect than per-

haps any other individual. Dr. Worcester died
in 1837, in the seventy-ninth year of his age. Of
his character Dr. Channing thus speaks :—
"Two views of him particularly impressed me.
The first was the unity, the harmony of his character. He had no jarring elements. His whole nature had been blended and melted into one strong,
serene love. His mission was to preach peace, and
he preached it, not on set occasions, or by separate
efforts, but in his whole life. .... And this seren-
ity was not the result of torpor or tameness, for his
whole life was a conflict with what he deemed error. He made no compromise with the world;
and yet he loved it as deeply and as constantly as
if it had responded in shouts to all his views and
feelings.

"The next great impression which I received
from him was that of the sufficiency of the mind to
its own happiness, or of its independence on outward things." Notwithstanding his poverty and
infirmities, "he spoke of his old age as among the
happiest portions, if not the very happiest, of his
life. In conversation, his religion manifested itself
more in gratitude than any other form." His voice
was cheerful, his look serene, and he devoted himself to his studies with youthful earnestness. "On
leaving his house, and turning my face toward this

city, 1 have said to myself, how much richer is this
poor man than the richest who dwell yonder! I
have been ashamed of my own dependence on outward good. I am always happy to express my ob-
ligations to the benefactors of my mind; and I owe
it to Dr. Worcester to say, that my acquaintance
with him gave me clearer comprehension of the
spirit of Christ and of the dignity of a man.

JAMES LACKINGTON,

A CELEBRATED bookseller of Finsbury Square,
London, and proprietor of the great bookselling
establishment there, which he called the " Temple
of the Muses," was born in 1746, and brought up
a shoemaker, at Wellington, in Shropshire. By
industry and perseverance he succeeded in the
bookselling business, almost beyond precedent.
On the publication of the seventh edition of his
memoirs, written by himself, in 1794, he had set
up his carriage, and his profits in each of the two
preceding years, were £5,000 (equal to $24,000).
He observes that —

> " Cobblers from Crispin boast their public spirit,
> And all are upright, downright men of merit."

Lackington mentions a brother shoemaker,
named Ralph Tilney, who died in 1789: " one who
had not dignity of birth or elevated rank in life to

boast of, but who possessed what is far superior to either, a solid understanding, amiable manners, a due sense of religion, and an industrious disposition. Among other acquisitions, entomology was his peculiar delight—his valuable cabinet of insects, both foreign and domestic, supposed to be one of the completest of a private collection in the kingdom, all scientifically arranged, with peculiar neatness, and in the finest preservation."

> " Honor and shame from no condition rise ;
> Act well your part, there all the honor lies."
> You 'll find if once the monarch acts the monk,
> Or. cobbler-like, the parson will get drunk,
> Worth makes the man, and want of it the fellow,
> The rest is all but leather or prunella.'

Lackington's memoirs bring his life down to 1793. His memoirs abound in severe remarks on the methodists (whom he had joined in early life and afterward left), both as to life, and doctrine; these Lackington subsequently repented having written. Uniting himself again to the Wesleyan society, he endeavored to obviate the injustice of his sarcasms by publishing a confession of his errors. Much of what he had stated, he acknowledged to have taken on trust; and many things he now discovered to have been without a proper foundation. These " Confessions," which appeared in 1803, never altogether accomplished their purpose; so

17*

difficult is it to recall or make reparation for a word
lightly spoken.   In sincere humiliation of spirit,
Lackington retired to Budleigh Sulterton, in Devonshire, where he built and endowed a chapel, and
performed various other acts of munificence, and
spent the conclusion of his days.   He died on the
22d of November, 1815, in the seventieth year of
his age.

JOSEPH PENDRELL.

JOSEPH PENDRELL, who died in London about
the year 1830, had received at school nothing more
than the ordinary education, in English reading and
writing.   At an early age he was apprenticed to a
shoemaker, which business he followed until his
death.   He had when young a great taste for books.
Stopping at a book-stall one day, he laid hold of a
an arithmetical work, marked four pence sterling;
he purchased it, and availed himself of his leisure
hours, in making himself master of the subject.
At the end of the volume he found a short introduction to mathematics ; this stimulated him to make
further purchases of scientific works; and in this
way he gradually proceeded from the elements to
the highest departments of mathematical learning.
When a journeyman, he made every possible saving in order to purchase books.   He subsequently

acquired a knowledge of French, Greek, and Latin, and formed a large collection of classical books, many of which he purchased at the auction-rooms, always concealing his name as purchaser. The late Bishop Lowth became interested in him, from occasional conversation at the auction sales, but the shoemaker, from extreme diffidence, declined telling his name, although the introduction to the bishop might have drawn him from his obscurity. Pendrell's knowledge of mathematical science, was profound and extensive, embracing fortification, navigation, astronomy, and various departments of natural philosophy. He was also familiar with poetical literature; and had a thorough acquaintance with most English writers in the department of *belles lettres.*

THOMAS HOLCROFT.

THOMAS HOLCROFT, an English miscellaneous writer of considerable reputation, was born in Orange court, Leicesterfields, December 22, 1744. His father was a shoemaker in low circumstances, and the son, early in life, was employed in the stables of the honorable Mr. Vernon. He also worked at his father's business of shoemaking, but being fond of reading, and his fellow-workmen sneering at his efforts to acquire knowledge, he left

the trade, and opened a school in London. This
not proving successful, he tried his fortune on the
stage, but after much suffering, being often almost
reduced to starvation, he abandoned the stage as an
actor. In the midst of his distresses, however, he
retained his love of books, and had made himself
extensively acquainted with English literature.

He then turned dramatic writer, in which he was
more fortunate, some of his plays being very popular at the time. Besides these productions, he
wrote several novels, and translated a number of
works from the French and German languages. At
the commencement of the French revolution, he
espoused the cause of the republicans, and was
committed for high treason; but when Hardy,
Tooke, and Thelwall, were acquitted, he was discharged, without trial. His last speculation was a
publication of his travels in Germany and France,
in two volumes quarto. Many of his works exhibit
high talents, and have an established popularity in
England. He died in 1809.

REV. WILLIAM CAREY, D. D.

THIS eminent Christian missionary, and distinguished oriental scholar, was born at Paulerspury,
Northamptonshire, England, in 1761. He followed
the business of shoemaking in early life, during

which time, he learned several languages, studying with his books by his side while at work. A gentleman in New York, has preserved in his library, among the works of Dr. Carey, a pair of shoes made by him.

Dr. Carey commenced preaching as a baptist minister in 1783; in 1793 he embarked as a missionary to India, and in 1799, he took up his residence at the Danish settlement of Serampore, which became celebrated for being the seat of this mission which was sustained by Carey, Ward, and Marshman.

Dr. Carey's philological labors in preparing grammars and dictionaries of different languages, and in making versions of the Scriptures, were immense. He lived to see the sacred Text, chiefly by his instrumentality, translated into the vernacular dialects of more than forty different tribes, and thus made accessible to nearly two hundred millions of human beings. In addition to his extensive philological learning, Dr. Carey was well versed in natural history and botany, and made valuable communications to the Asiatic society, of which he was for twenty-eight years a member. He died at Serampore, in Hindostan, June 9, 1834, in his seventy-third year.

GEORGE FOX.

GEORGE Fox, the founder and first preacher of
the Christian sect of Friends, or Quakers, was born
at Drayton, Leicestershire, England, in 1624. He
was bound by his father, who was a weaver, to a
shoemaker and grazier; and the occupation of his
youth was divided between shoemaking and the
tending of sheep. He did not, however, long follow either of these occupations, as, in 1643, he
began his wandering life; and, after retiring to sol-
itude, and at other times frequenting the company
of religious and devout persons, he became a public
preacher in 1647 or 1648. In his pious zeal, Fox
visited, not only England, Ireland, and Scotland,
but he extended his travels to Holland and Germany, to the American colonies and the West India
islands. He died in London, in 1690. His journal was printed in 1694, his epistles in 1698, his
doctrinal pieces, about one hundred and fifty in
number, in 1706. The name of quakers was first
given to him and his followers, at Derby, in England.

REV. JAMES NICHOL.

JAMES NICHOL, of Traquair, Selkirkshire, Scotland, was the son of a shoemaker, and he also learn-

ed the same trade of his father, and continued to labor at it, in the summer vacations, after he had entered college. With the manners of a gentleman, Mr. Nichol possessed uncommon talents. He was a most able and eloquent pulpit orator; an eminent scholar; and an acute, ingenious, and liberal theologian. In early life he published two or three volumes of poems, of considerable celebrity. He wrote several articles in one of the encyclopedias, and in various periodicals; and left a number of theological and literary works for publication.

REV. WILLIAM HUNTINGTON.

This late celebrated and popular preacher of Providence chapel, Gray's Inn lane, London, worked for some time as a shoemaker, as he informs us, in his "Bank of Faith," a work singularly curious and interesting.

CHAPTER IX.

HAVING given, in the preceding chapter, bio-graphical sketches of some of the sons of St. Crispin, who have risen from the *last*, to the first rank among their fellow-men, in the several departments of knowledge, we shall conclude this work with a few anecdotes, and such matters as are of interest to the craft in general.

PATRON SAINTS OF THE SHOEMAKERS.—Crispin and Crispianus were brethren, born at Rome, from which city they travelled to Soissons, in France, for the purpose of propagating the Christian religion, A. D., 303; and in order that they might not be chargeable to others for their maintenance, they exercised the trade of shoemakers; but Rectionarius, governor of the town, discovering them to be Christians, condemned them to be beheaded; hence they became the tutelar saints of the shoemakers.

The following singular passage with reference to

the preservation of the relics of these saints, occurs in Lusius's Acts of the Martyrs, where he notices the blessed Crispin and Crispianus. After their execution, their bodies, according to our author, were cast out to be devoured by dogs and birds of prey : nevertheless, being protected by the power of Christ, they suffered no harm. During the same night in which they were martyred, a certain indigent old man, who resided with his aged sister, was warned by an angel to take the bodies of these holy martyrs, and to deposite them, with all proper care, in a sepulchre. The old man, without hesitation, arose, and, accompanied by his venerable sister, went to the place where the bodies of the martyrs lay. As this was near the river Arona, they could easily, with the assistance of a small boat, have brought them to their own dwelling; this, however, on account of their poverty and infirmity, they were unable to procure, nor, indeed, had they any experience in the management of a vessel, which, moreover, must have been rowed against the current. When, however, after diligently searching in the dark, they at last found the precious corpses wholly uninjured—lo! they discovered a small boat close to the shore, and thereupon assuming courage immediately, they each took up a body, so staggering under the weight from weakness, that they appear

18

not so much to carry their burdens as to be carried by them. Placing the bodies in the boat, they floated with great celerity against the current of the river, and, without the assistance of either rudder or oars, presently arrived at their own cottage ; near to which, with equal secresy and joy, they interred the bodies of the deceased martyrs.

In Soissons, there are many churches and religious places dedicated to these saints. There is a tradition of their interment in England.

St. Crispin's Day.—Crispin stands marked in our almanacs for remembrance, on the 25th of October, though his brother, Crispianus or Crispinian, appears to have an equal claim to that respect. Their history is only imperfectly known, and affords nothing particularly interesting beyond the preceding notice. In an old romance, a prince of the name of Crispin is represented as having exercised the profession of a shoemaker; and thence is supposed to be derived the expression of the " gentle craft," as applied to that art :—

> " Our shoes were sewed with merry notes,
> And by our mirth expelled all moan ;
> Like nightingales, from whose sweet throats
> Most pleasant tunes are nightly blown :
> The Gentle Craft is fittest then
> For poor distressèd gentlemen."

The immortal Shakspere has given a speech to Henry the Fifth, before the battle of Agincourt, that will mark the anniversary of St. Crispin to the latest posterity:—

" This day is called — the feast of Crispian:
He, that outlives this day, and comes safe home,
Will stand a tiptoe when this day is named,
And rouse him at the name of Crispian :
He, that shall live this day, and see old age,
Will yearly on the vigil feast his friends,
And say, To-morrow is St. Crispian:
Then will he strip his sleeve and show his scars.
Old men forget; yet shall not all forget,
But they'll remember with advantages,
What feats they did that day: Then shall our names,
Familiar in their mouth as household words,—
Harry the king, Bedford, and Exeter,
Warwick, and Talbot, Salisbury, and Glo'ster,—
Be in their flowing cups freshly remembered :
This story shall the good man teach his son :
And Crispin Crispian shall ne'er go by,
From this day to the ending of the world,
But we in it shall be remembered :
We few, we happy few, we band of brothers;
For he to-day that sheds his blood with me,
Shall be my brother; be he ne'er so vile,
This day shall gentle his condition :
And gentlemen in England, now abed,
Shall think themselves accursed they were not here;
And hold their manhoods cheap, while any speaks
That fought with us upon St. Crispin's day."

CORDWAINERS' HALL is a modern structure, situated in Distaff lane, London. It is, a plain, but very neat and substantial brick building, with a stone front, and a sculpture of the cordwainers' arms, on a shield, in the pediment, supported on each side by the cornucopia, or horn of plenty. Over the centre window is a bass-relief of Clotho, one of the parcæ or fates, spinning the thread of life,

The hall is entered by two side-wings, by an ascent of a few steps. On the right and left are rooms for counting-houses, and other offices for the use of the clerks and different persons belonging to the company. The ballroom, 60 feet by 30, is a neat, commodious room, but without ornaments, except merely the royal arms, the city arms, and the arms of the company. Over the entrance is a music gallery or orchestra, underneath which are some extremely neat representations of musical instruments.

The court-room, 30 feet by 15, is a very neat room, the walls hung with various plans of estates belonging to the company. Over the fireplace is a beautiful engraved view of the hall, drawn by Mr. Michael Meredith. The view is taken from the southwest angle, and gives a correct view, in perspective, of the west entrance, as well as of the front. Opposite this picture, at the other end of the room, is another view of the hall, an entire front view, showing both the wings. This was drawn by Mr. Robinson, of Lothbury, surveyor to the company. Over this room is the smoking-room, a perfectly plain, but clean and neat apartment. Opposite to this is the dining-room, at the east end of which is a capital picture, by Sir William Beechy, of William Williams, Esq., who, after being three times elected master of the company, died on the 5th of November, 1809, aged eighty-seven. The portrait is very large, and painted in Beechy's best style. The frame is superbly gilt and ornamented. It is surmounted by Mr. Williams's own arms. At the other end of this room, are the arms of the company, richly emblazoned. Under this, in a niche, is a massy sepulchred urn, of white marble, on a base of the same material, bearing the following inscription :—

" This tablet is dedicated to the memory of Mr. John Carne, many years a valuable member of this company, in testimony of the many virtues which adorned his character, particularly that spirit of benevolence and charity so manifestly displayed in his last will, dated the 12th of August, 1782, by which he gave, in trust, to the master, wardens, and stewards of this company for ever, £37,200

18*

three per cent. government annuities, the interest arising therefrom he bequeathed to this company, and also subject to certain annuities, amounting to £145, to be by them annually distributed in £5 each, to clergymen's widows. Mr. Carne died the 13th of May, 1796, aged seventy-eight years, and was buried in the church of St. Mary-le-bow, London. Mr. Carne, during several years prior to his death, gave £300 for the same purposes as those mentioned on the tablet."

On one side of this room is a neat music gallery. There are, besides, several other minor apartments, and beneath, a most excellent kitchen, with all sorts of culinary apparatus.

INCORPORATED SHOEMAKERS.—When and where the shoemakers first began to form themselves into societies, and to observe the festival of their saint, does not appear; it is natural enough to suppose that the celebrity of Crispin and Crispianus, would confer on the day and place an honor, which they who wrought at the same occupation would wish to record and celebrate; at Soissons, therefore, it is probable that a trade, which had been selected and distinguished by saints and martyrs, would be also distinguished by some principles of recognition by its members. Be this as it may, it is certain that the memory of the above saints is honored in the city of their decollation, where churches, and other religious buildings, are dedicated to "St. Crispin," "St. Crispin the Greater," "St. Crispin the Less," "St. Crispin *en chay*," &c.

In Paris, there are two pious societies, with the title of "*Freres Cordonniers*," or brothers shoemakers. They were established by authority, about the middle of the sixteenth century; the one under the patronage of St. Crispin, and the other of Crispianus. They live in community, and are governed by fixed statutes and officers, both in their secular and spiritual concerns. The produce of the shoes which they make goes to the common stock, to furnish necessaries for their support, the overplus to be distributed among the poor.

Shoemakers are legally called cordwainers, or cordovanners, from Cordova, a town and province in Spain, whence the leather called cordovan was brought. The Latin appellation of a shoemaker is SUTOR or CALCEOLARIUS, in Greek it is PAΠTHΣ, in Arabic SABBATERO, in French CORDINNIER. The cordwainer's company was first incorporated in England by the letters patent of Henry IV., in the year 1410, by the style of the "Cordwainer's and Cobbler's Company." The incorporation of this

body was again recognised early in the fifteenth
century, by an act of parliament, the provisions of
which were to restrict the making of boots, shoes,
&c., after a certain "preposterous" fashion then
prevalent: defaults to be adjudged by the wardens
of the company, and a fine of twenty shillings to
be levied on the party so offending. A like pen-
alty was inflicted by the same act upon any "cordwainer or cobbler," in London, or within three
miles of it, who should be convicted of making, or
putting upon the legs or feet of any person, any
shoes, boots, or buskins, on *Sundays*, or feasts of
the nativity and ascension of our Lord, and Corpus
Christi. Shoemakers are incorporated in Edin-
burgh, and called CORDINERS.

PROVERBS.—Several common and proverbial ex-
pressions are taken from the shoemaker's trade.
"To stick to the last," is used of perseverance in
an undertaking till its completion. "Nothing is
like leather," signifies to cry up one's own craft, as
in the case of the currier, who would have defend-
ed the town with tanned cowhides. "*Urit pedem
calceus*," I am in the shoemaker's stocks. "*Ne sutor ultra crepidam*," the shoemaker must not go
beyond his last. These were the words of Apel-

les, a famous painter of antiquity, to a critical Crispin, who properly found fault with an ill-designed
slipper. The artist amended his picture accordingly; but the cobbler, ascending to other parts,
betrayed the grossest ignorance. "No man," says
a commentator on this proverb, "should pass his
opinion in a province of art where he is without a
qualification."—"*Etre sur un grand pied dans le
monde*," to be on a great foot (or footing) in the
world. This favorite French proverb originated at
the time when a man's rank was known by the
size of his shoes. Those of a prince measured
two feet and a half; a plain cit was allowed only
twelve inches. A noble Roman being asked why
he had put away his beautiful wife, put forth his
foot, and showed his buskins. "Is not this," said
he, "a handsome and complete shoe? yet no man
but myself knows where it pinches me." Hence
the saying, "None but the wearer knows where the
shoe pinches." As "tight as a bristle," is still a
common saying of anything that is attached dexter-
ously, or that fits nicely, and is derived from the
exactness required by the cobbler in fixing a bristle
to the thread or *end* with which he sews, that it may
follow the awl the better. The waxed string pointed with bristle, as at present, was in use as early
as the twelfth century.

THE following pleasant anecdote used to be told by the eccentric Dr. Monsey. The duke of Leeds, the doctor, and his grace's chaplain, being one morning, soon after breakfast, in his library, Mr. Walkden, of Pall Mall, his grace's shoemaker, was shown in with a pair of new shoes for the duke. The latter was remarkably fond of him, as he was at the same time clerk of St. James's church, where the duke was a constant attendant. "What have you there, Walkden?" said the duke.—"A pair of shoes for your grace," he replied.—"Let me see them." They were handed to him accordingly. The chaplain taking up one of them examined it with great attention : "What is the price?" asked the chaplain. "Half a guinea, sir," said the shoemaker. "Half a guinea! what for a pair of shoes?" said the chaplain. "Why I could go to Cranbourn alley, and buy a better pair of shoes than they ever were or ever will be, for five and sixpence." He then threw the shoe to the other end of the room. Walkden threw the other after it, saying as they were fellows they ought to go together; and at the same time replied to the chaplain : "Sir, I can go to a stall in Moorfields and buy a better sermon for twopence, than my lord gives you a guinea for." The duke clapped Walkden on the shoulder, and said, "That is a

most excellent retort, Walkden; make me half a
dozen pairs of shoes directly."

THE greatest multitude of shoemakers ever
known to have been assembled on one occasion,
were collected by the celebrated mob-orator, Hen-
ley, at his oratory near Lincoln's-Inn-Fields. This
public declaimer used to discourse on general topics during the week, and on some subject of moral-
ity on the Sunday. On the above occasion he had
announced that on a given day he should discourse
to shoemakers, and that he could teach them a
most expeditious method of making shoes—which
proved to be no other than cutting off the tops of
ready-made boots! The admission ticket on that
occasion bore the following motto : "Omne majus
continet in se minus." The writer of this anecdote says : " I can not think the representatives of
Prince Crispin would have pocketed this insult. I
think they would have *bristled* up, one and *all*, and,
waxing wroth, would not have waited for the
ends of justice, but would have brought the orator
down from his 'gilt tub,' and persevering to the
last, have put their *soles* upon his neck till he had
discovered too late, that the 'gentle craft,' might
not be insulted with impunity."

A SHOEMAKER attending a public ball, where he happened to be the handsomest and best-dressed gentleman, the mushroom gentry thought to play a trick on him. While engaged in a dance, a stocking manufacturer begged to be measured for a pair of boots, to be ready by five o'clock next morning. The shoemaker, observing his drift, and the approbation of a considerable part of the company, immediately desired him to hold it on the floor, and with one knee on it measured the foot: then saying, "You may depend upon it, the boots will be ready according to your order;" he ordered half a dozen pairs of silk stockings, to be ready at the same hour, and proceeded with the dance. Having stayed till two o'clock in the morning, he waked some of his workmen, and had the boots finished by five o'clock; then sending and obliging the stocking manufacturer to rise, and try on his boots, which exactly fitted, he ordered instant payment of five guineas for them, and threatened prosecution, as the stockings were not ready according to promise.

THE END.

CPSIA information can be obtained
at www.ICGtesting.com
Printed in the USA
BVHW081408260122
627129BV00019B/1389